W9-BYZ-702

Trinidad & Tobago

Don Philpott

Acknowledgements

My sincere thanks to everyone who helped me research and write this book and who made the project even more enjoyable. In particular, my very special thanks to Cliff Hamilton, Director of Tourism, Patrice Ammon, Sandra Hendrickson, and Tony Poyer for his good company and encyclopaedic knowledge.

Dedication: To Pam, my beautiful American Rose

Florida

Miami

Bahamas

TRINIDAD & TOBAGO

Florida Keys

Atlantic
Ocean

CUBA

Dominican
Republic

Puerto
Rico

Jamaica

N

W ●●●● E

S

Caribbean Sea

TOBAGO

Venezuela

TRINIDAD

Trinidad & Tobago

Don Philpott

• FEATURE BOXES •

Trinidad and Tobago is a delightful two-island nation that offers the best the Caribbean has to offer. Trinidad is a large, lively, cosmopolitan island with lots of attractions and the home of Carnival, calypso and steel bands, while Tobago is a small, laid back island, and the perfect place to get away from it all and simply enjoy the sun, sea and sand. Both islands offer spectacular and stunning scenery, and a huge range of plant and animal life, on land and in the sea. There are hotels and restaurants to suit all tastes and pockets, festivals and carnivals, historic buildings and sights, botanical gardens and parks, and above all, magnificent palm-tree lined beaches, golden sands and warm, turquoise seas.

Hot Spots

Trinidad
- Maracas Bay
- Asa Wright Nature Reserve
- Nariva Swamp
- Caroni Swamp
- Port of Spain – Savannah and area

Tobago
- Buccoo Reef
- Little Tobago
- Mt Irvine Bay for surfing
- Tobago Museum at Fort King George

GEOGRAPHY

Trinidad and Tobago (Toe-bay-go) are the southernmost of the Caribbean islands lying only 7 miles (10km) off the north-east coast of South America, to the north-east of Venezuela, and to the north-west of Guyana, and were once connected to the mainland. Trinidad is the largest of the Lesser Antilles, but unlike the other Caribbean islands in the chain, it is not volcanic, although Tobago is. The two islands are 21 miles (33km) apart, and together have a total area of 1,978 sq miles (5146sq km). Trinidad is the larger of the two, covering 1,864 sq miles (4849 sq km), and Port-of-Spain in the north west of the island, is the capital. It is roughly rectangular in shape, 50 miles (80km) long and 37 miles (60km) wide. Trinidad is just 7 miles (11km) at the nearest point from the Venezuelan coast and separated from it by the Gulf of Paria and two channels strewn with several islands and rocks.

Tobago covers an area of 116 sq miles (302 sq km), and lies 21 miles

(33km) to the north-east in the Atlantic Ocean. It is almost exactly half way between the island of Grenada and the Venezuelan coastline. At its longest, from north-east to south-west, it is 32 miles (52km) across, and is 11 miles (18km) across at its widest. Little Tobago, also known as Bird of Paradise Island, is one mile (1.6km) off Tobago's north east coast, and gets its name because outside of New Guinea, it was until 1963, the only known wild habitat of the greater bird of paradise.

Geologically, the islands are an extension of the South American continent, and Trinidad's most outstanding feature is the Northern Range, which is a continuation of coastal foothills of the Andes Mountains in Venezuela. The range, averaging 1,500ft (457m), runs from west to east along the north coast and its highest point is Aripo Mountain at 3,085ft (940m). The mountains are beautiful and spectacularly rich in plant and wildlife. There are also many waterfalls in the mountains, the largest of which are the Blue Basin and the Maracas Falls, both plunging for almost 300ft (91m). There is a central plain with rolling hills to the south, and half the island is forested.

On the southern side of the range, the mountains fall away to foothills that run to the northern plain. The central plain has a ridge of hills, the highest point of which is Mount Tamana 1,009ft (308m), while there is a third chain of low hills running along the south.

The three areas of upland dictate Trinidad's drainage system, and while there are many rivers, they are generally short and often fan out into swampland in lower areas. The longest rivers are the Ortoire in the south that runs for 31 miles (50km), and the Caroni that flows for 25 miles (40km) in the north, part of it through the Caroni swamp.

A feature of part of the south are mud volcanoes, caused by gas and water seepage, part of an oil-bearing belt that runs through the southern part of the island, west into the Gulf of Paria and east into the Atlantic Ocean. The most famous of these volcanoes is the Devil's Woodyard, and in the south-west of the island, there is Pitch Lake, a sedimentary volcano, the crater of which holds reserves of asphalt.

Tobago geologically is an extension of the Andean coastal chain and the mountains of Trinidad. It has a central spine, Main Ridge that runs from north-east to south-west, rising to 1,860ft (549m) at its highest point. The ridge slopes gently to the south-west on to a rich coral plain. The offshore reefs are rich in marine life and popular dive sites. There are no rivers on Tobago and only a few short streams.

A LITTLE HISTORY....

The original people of the islands were the gentle Arawaks, an Amerindian race, although relatively little is known about them or when they first arrived. They are believed to have come from Asia to the Orinoco region of South America about 40,000 years ago. They fished, hunted and grew plants such as maize, tobacco and cassava, but food was plentiful and they had lots of time to lie in the sun and party! They lived in small coastal communities, wore few clothes but decorated themselves with tattoos, feathers and beads, and were skilled potters.

They called Trinidad Iere, which meant the land of hummingbirds.

Warlike Caribs, another Amerindian race, certainly landed on Trinidad some time between AD800 and 1000, but it is thought they did not permanently settle and moved on in their huge war canoes to colonize other islands in the Caribbean where in most cases, they virtually eradicated the Arawaks. There are, however, people living in Arima, Trinidad's oldest community, who proudly claim to be directly descended from Carib royalty.

There is evidence of both an Arawak and Carib presence on Tobago, but it is not known whether either were permanent settlers on the island before Columbus.

It is known that the Caribs had a well-developed social system and common language throughout the Caribbean islands. Hereditary kings (*Caciques*) ruled while *shamans* were the religious leaders. Their reputation as warriors was fearsome, and their war canoes could hold more than a hundred men able to paddle fast enough to catch a sailing ship. They were feared by Europeans because of horrific stories about cannibalism with victims being roasted on spits. The Caribs were even said to have a taste preference, thinking Frenchmen were the tastiest, and then the English and Dutch, with the Spanish considered stringy and almost inedible.

Villages were built in inland forest clearings, and each settlement had its own chieftain. Huts were round with timber walls and palm thatched roofs. Early paintings show that they enjoyed dancing, either for pleasure or as part of rituals, and they played ball games. They were primarily fishermen and hunt-

ers, although they did cultivate kitchen gardens, and developed a system of shift cultivation, known as *conuco* The early Spanish recorded their surprise at the Arawak's agricultural techniques, use of fibers for weaving and pottery and boat-building skills.

Columbus names Trinidad

Trinidad and Tobago were 'discovered' by Columbus in 1498 during his Third Voyage. He named the larger island Trinidad (Spanish for the Trinity) because when it first appeared on the horizon he spotted three large hills which to him symbolized the three elements of the Holy Trinity.

Many of the Arawaks living on Trinidad were captured by Spanish slavers and sent to work in Spanish possessions in the Caribbean.

The Spanish did not attempt to settle Trinidad until 1592 when Antonio de Berrio founded St. Joseph as the island's capital. For 200 years it was the only European settlement on the island. With greater riches offered in Cuba, Hispaniola and Puerto Rico to the north, few Spaniards chose to settle on Trinidad and so few slaves were needed. In the seventeenth and early-eighteenth century tobacco and cacao were the main crops with the plantations manned mostly by Amerindians. In 1720 the cacao crop failed and for almost 50 years the island stagnated until 1776 when the Spanish government encouraged Roman Catholics from other Caribbean posses-

Continued on page 12...

CLIMATE ON THE ISLANDS

Best time to go

Any time is a good time to visit the islands. The high season is generally regarded as between mid-November and March which is also the driest time, but the island now attracts visitors by air and from cruise ships year round. Most rain falls between May and October.

Climate

The islands enjoy a brillant climate and even when it does rain, it is warm rain and generally does not last long. The islands lie within the tropical zone in the path of the north-east trade winds and have a typical sub tropical maritime climate of year-round sunny, warm weather. Temperatures along the coast are moderated by the onshore sea breezes.

Temperatures remain fairly constant throughout the year, with only a few degrees fluctuation between summer and winter. Average temperatures throughout the year are generally within the range of 77°F (25°C) in February, and 85°F (29°C) in April. The average daytime temperatures are around 83°F (29°C) and average night temperatures around 65°F (18°C). During the hottest part of the year, however, temperatures some days can often be in the high nineties, and humidity can be high.

The coolest months are January and February when the temperature averages about 68°F (20°C), and the warmest months are April, May and October, which have an average maximum temperature of 89°F (32°C). Tobago tends to be slightly cooler and less humid than Trinidad.

The dry season lasts from January to May, but do not be fooled into thinking it does not rain during these months, and the wet season is from May to December, although there is often an Indian Summer, the Petit Careme, in September and October. When it does rain, it tends to pour but in short, sharp bursts. Annual rainfall is about 70 inches (175cm), but higher in the rain forest. Even if you get soaked, the rain rarely lasts long and the sun quickly dries you.

Hurricanes

The islands are outside the general hurricane belt that runs to the north, but Tobago has been hit twice in the last 150 years – in 1867 and 1963.

Hurricane season in the Caribbean lasts from June to November with September and October usually the busiest months for tropical storms. If a hurricane should threaten, follow the advice given locally.

Above: View over Blue Water Inn Bay, Tobago
Below: Coconut plantation, Cocos Bay, Trinidad

sions to settle on Trinidad with their slaves. In 1783 immigration was boosted further by a Royal decree (*Cedula*) offering generous land grants. Many of the new wave of settlers were French Catholics or of French descent – escaping the French Revolution at home or slave uprisings in Saint Domingue which is now Haiti – and they established huge plantations which required large numbers of slaves to be brought in, both from other Caribbean islands and from Africa.

Within ten years, the island's population rocketed and by the time Britain seized Trinidad from Spain in February 1797, it had a firmly established plantation economy based on a slave workforce. The Spanish Governor Chacon surrendered the island but sank his five ships in the port rather than hand them over, and Picton became the first British Governor. By the end of the eighteenth century Trinidad was in British hands but was largely French speaking and still operating under Spanish laws but was a lawless island. Gallows were erected and a ruthless regime was introduced to restore law and order. In 1814, England's possession of Trinidad was formally identified.

During this period, thousands of slaves were brought to the islands from West Africa to man the sugar cane plantations. The infamous Triangular trade was introduced – sugar and molasses from the West Indies was sent to European ports, and the money from their sale was used to buy slaves, who were sold in the West Indies for sugar.

Britain abolished the slave trade in 1807, and in 1834 all slavery was abolished in the British West Indies. After Emancipation, however, all former slaves had to agree to serve a four-year 'apprenticeship'. They had to agree to work free for their former bosses for at last three quarters of their working week. The rest of the time could be spent tending small plots cleared from the forest on which crops were grown.

Without a cheap labor force following the 'apprenticeship', the plantations faced ruin, so in 1845, the owners introduced 'indentured' workers from the East Indies, China and Portugal, and this policy continued until 1917 during which time almost 150,000 Indians had come to Trinidad. Originally they received only food and board in return for a grant of 5 acres (2 hectares) of land at the end of their 'indentures', usually seven or nine years. By 1870, one in four of the island's population was Indian, but immigration from many other countries since the 1830s, made Trinidad the most mixed community in the Caribbean.

Columbus is also credited for discovering Tobago in 1498 but the island remained virtually untouched by Europeans until 1763 when it was ceded to Britain. English settlers quickly established sugar cane plantations but the next fifty years were troubled, with the island fought over by Britain and France, changing hands several times. In fact, Holland and Spain also claimed and occupied Tobago at various times, and altogether the island changed hands twenty-two times.

Despite the turmoil, Tobago became the richest sugar cane island in the Caribbean although by 1814 when Tobago was ceded to Britain for the last time, the sugar cane industry was already in decline. By 1888 with its economy shattered, Tobago was amalgamated with

Trinidad in a single administrative unit.

Polyglot community

The diversity of the immigrant population is shown in the many languages used for place names. The Spanish settled at Sangre Grande, San Fernando and Port of Spain, the French immigrants named Sans Souci, Matelot and Blanchisseuse, the British established Scarborough, Plymouth and Roxborough, while the original settlers, the Arawaks are remembered by place names such as Guayaguayare, Tunapuna and Cocorite.

Constitutional changes in 1925 and greater representation did not satisfy calls for reform, and after island-wide strikes and riots in 1937, universal suffrage and major reforms were introduced in 1946, although for the next ten years politics were dominated by individuals rather than parties. In 1956 the People's National Movement (PNM) formed the first cabinet-based government with Eric Williams as Prime Minister, and two years later Trinidad and Tobago joined the Federation of the West Indies. An indication of the political influence held by Trinidad and Tobago in the Caribbean was that Chaguaramas was chosen as the site for the Caribbean Parliament, although building work did not start. They remained members until 1962 when the Federation was dissolved and in the same year Trinidad and Tobago achieved independence from Britain, and in 1976, became a republic within the Commonwealth. The Tobago House of Assembly was established in 1980. The PNM governed until the general election of 1986 when the coalition National Alliance for Reconstruction (NAR) came to power under Arthur Robinson. The PNM was returned to power in 1991 but was defeated when Prime Minister Patrick Manning went to the country a year early in 1995, and a coalition of the United National Congress (UNC) and the NAR came to power, and UNC leader Basdeo Panday, became the first Trinidadian of Indian descent to be sworn in as Prime Minister.

THE PEOPLE

The islands have a population of about 1.25 million of whom 350,000 live in and around Port of Spain and 45,000 on Tobago. The census of 1861 showed a population of less than 100,000. Other major urban areas in Trinidad are San Fernando in the south, Chaguanas in the west, and Arima in the east. Scarborough is the main settlement and market town of Tobago. Architectural styles vary from the typical rural huts with thatched or tin roofs, to brightly painted two floor homes with their ornate gingerbread fretwork, and the Spanish-influenced buildings that can still be seen in Port of Spain.

The islanders have their roots in many parts of the world, particularly Africa, India, Europe, the Mediterranean, Middle East and China, all of whom introduced their own languages, cultures, religions and cuisines, and this accounts for

Above: A stall of leather products, Sandy Bay, Tobago
Below: House at Speyside, Tobago

Trinidad's remarkable cosmopolitan atmosphere. Tobago's population is mainly of African descent.

RELIGIONS AND RELIGIOUS FESTIVALS

About 29 per cent of the population is Roman Catholic, a legacy of Spanish colonial rule, bolstered by French immigrants during the French and Haitian Revolutions. About a quarter of the population is Hindu, eleven per cent Anglican, and six per cent Muslim. The others belong to a wide number of religious groups including Baptist, Moravian, Presbyterian, Methodist, evangelical denominations and traditional African faiths, such as the Orisha, Shango and Shouter cults.

Orisha stems from the religious beliefs of the Yoruba people, originally from south-west Nigeria, in which there is a complex hierarchy of Gods, ascending in importance to the Supreme Creator. Every year a ceremony is performed to praise the water god Yemonja.

There are many other religious festivals reflecting the diverse beliefs and traditions. These include various forms of *pooja* (or *puja*), which involve ceremonial offerings, and the Divali or the Festival of Lights that is an important event in November. It symbolizes the triumph of light over darkness, and during the festival, thousands of *deyas* (clay pots with oil-fueled wicks) are lit in homes and public places. The main venue for public observance of the festival is at Divali Nagar in central Trinidad. The festival, however, is not just enjoyed by Hindus but is island-wide as homes are thrown open so that friendship and hospitality can be shared.

The bright flags seen in many front gardens, especially in the central region, are Hindu prayer flags, and each variation represents a different God being worshipped.

At Christmas, groups of Christian singers stroll the streets. These are the paranderos, the Trinidadian version of carolers, and their parang music is sung in the original Spanish to the accompaniment of cuatros.

Rastafarianism

There are also significant numbers of Rastafarians on Trinidad and many are talented craftsmen. Rastafarianism originated in Jamaica and gave birth to the distinctive national music called reggae, popularized worldwide by the late Bob Marley. There is no doubt that Rastafarianism is largely misunderstood, partly perhaps because of the appearance of many of its adherents who, for religious reasons, wear their hair in dreadlocks. Rastafarians are generally young, peace-loving, teetotal vegetarians, who worship the Black Messiah. Their spiritual leader is the late Emperor Haile Selassie of Ethiopia, who they believe is still with them, and whose title includes 'ras' meaning prince and 'tafari' meaning 'to be feared'. They believe they are one of the lost tribes of Israel and that Ethiopia is the Promised Land. They do not smoke tobacco but many use 'sacred' *ganja* (hashish), which they smoke from a pipe called a chalice, reinforcing the religious symbolism attached to it. Most prefer to commune with nature and avoid the tourist areas, but there are many Rasta imitators who try to hustle for money, so be warned.

ARTS, CULTURE AND ENTERTAINMENT

The islanders have a natural artistry that is evidenced by the wonderfully woven baskets, rugs and hats, decorated pots and ornate jewels, often using natural material such as seeds. This artistic ability has been handed down over scores of generations, with even the earliest Arawak ceramics showing ornate patterns and designs. Canoe building and basket weaving are skills passed down ever since the Arawaks.

Music is an essential part of life in Trinidad and Tobago from Carnival and steel pans to calypso and jazz. There is folk singing and dancing and there is even a lilt and rhythm in the way the people speak.

The East Indian Culture Festival takes place every April in San Fernando in Skinner Park and showcases music, song and dance. Penal is known for the Shiv Shakti dancers, and the Nrityanjali Theatre dance group performs classical Indian dance.

There is a range of theaters in Trinidad. It is the home of the world-famous Trinidad Theatre Workshop founded in 1959 by Derek Walcott, the Nobel Laureate. The company performs many of Walcott's own works, and he often directs productions.

In contrast, there is the Space Theater that specializes in comedies and light hearted, and often irreverent looks at Trinidadian life. A visit to the Space Theatre is an occasion not to be missed because apart from the production itself, the exuberance and good-nature of the audience is a per-formance in its own right.

The Creative Arts Centre on the campus of the University of the West Indies also stages a wide range of productions from avant-garde to experimental local works. There are several other venues in Port of Spain where you can enjoy fringe theatre including Under The Trees at the Hotel Normandie, Cafédes Artistes, and Planteurs.

Queen's Hall stages calypso musicals and almost every other sort of musical performance from the classics to opera and ballet. It is also the venue for the National Dance Association's annual season. Also of note are the Noble Douglas Dance Company and the Trinidad Tent Theater.

Annual Best Village Competition

Among the best of the many troupes of folk dancers are the Trinidad Folk Performers, and the best place to see the cream of the islands' dancers is at the finals of the Best Village Competition that takes place in November at the Grandstand in Queen's Park Savannah. Communities also compete in song and arts and crafts, and it is a great place to sample traditional island fare from the many food stalls.

Apart from the excellent national art gallery, there are a number of private art galleries in Port of Spain which feature the works – paintings, sculptures and other art forms – by leading Trinidadian artists such as LeRoy Clarke, Ken Crichlow, Jackie Hinkson, Lisa O'Connor and Isaiah

MAJOR FESTIVALS ON THE ISLANDS

Phagwa which is a joyous Hindu New Year ceremony when celebrants sing their *chowtal* songs and squirt each other with abeer, a purple-dyed water – it is used as a food coloring and washes out. It is a sort of Hindu mini-Carnival with bands, floats, dancing and street parties. The main celebrations are held in Aranguez, Chaguanas, Penal Town and Princes Town.

Eid ul Fitr is the beginning of the Islamic New Year and coincides with the end of Ramadan, the holy month of fasting.

Easter is the first Christian festival of the year, and apart from the religious ceremonies, there are crab and goat races at Buccoo on Tobago, and beauty queen pageants.

Hosay is an important Muslim Festival that takes place over four days in May or June. Originally it was a very solemn affair commemorating the deaths of Hassan and Hussein, the grandsons of the prophet Mohammed during the Holy War of Kerbala. It is held at the end of a month of fasting during which bright *tadjahs,* representations of the tombs of the brothers, are built. The tombs are central to the festival. On the first night, flags representing different Muslim deities are paraded through the streets, small *tadjahs* are paraded on the second night, the full size *tadjahs* are paraded on the third night, and the festival culminates on the fourth night with hypnotic tassa-drumming and the ritualistic casting of the tombs into the sea.

The **Tobago Heritage Festivals** usually held over the last two weeks of July, is a commemoration of the island's past, and includes a wide range of activities from dining on traditional dishes to story telling, and being able to witness ancient fishermen's ceremonial customs and plantation celebrations. There are also art exhibitions, arts and crafts, musical performances and street parades.

The **Santa Rosa Festival** takes place in Arima in August, when the community commemorates its proud Carib heritage, and the life of Rosa de Lima, the first Amerindian to be canonized by the Catholic Church. Each year a Carib Queen is elected to head the parade through the town.

The **Pan Jazz Festival** is held in November and brings together top musicians from the worlds of pan and jazz, and displays the versatility of the pan both as a solo instrument and an ensemble instrument in the jazz medium.

Boodhoo. Trinidad has produced many internationally acclaimed writers, including C. L. R. James, Samuel Selvon and V V S Naipaul.

And, bridging the gap between culture and entertainment is cricket, played by almost everyone, anytime and anywhere. If you get the chance, go and watch a match being played at the Queen's Park Oval Cricket

Ground, it is an art form in itself and an experience you will never forget.

ECONOMY

The islands' economy is primarily based on petroleum, with tourism and manufacturing industries of growing importance. Extensive new major oil and gas field finds on land and at sea, guarantee the islands' economic growth in the short term although there is high unemployment. The islands also have significant deposits of argillite, asphalt, coal, fluorspar, gypsum, iron ore, limestone, sand and gravel. Natural gas has also been found off the coasts of Trinidad and Tobago. Oil production and refining is the main industry, although a Government-sponsored policy of diversification has been introduced. These new industries include assembly plants covering a wide range of consumer products from automobiles to televisions and electrical goods, and the production of fertilizer, cement, paper products, clothing, furniture and processed foods.

Most of the cultivated land is divided into small farms of a few acres and agriculture is not a major economic sector. The main export crops are sugar, cocoa and coffee, although coconuts, citrus, rice, poultry and vegetables are grown.

Manufacturing has traditionally been based on processing agricultural produce, but was diversified after Hurricane Allen with the construction of factories to produce electrical components, cardboard cartons, clothing, rum, tobacco products, coconut products, beer and concrete blocks.

Tourism continues to grow in economic importance, especially on Tobago. The number of hotel rooms on the island is expected to almost double over the next five years to reach 3,000, at which point it is likely to be capped to maintain the quality of the destination. The number of cruise passenger arrivals is also expected to double by the year 2001 to about 60,000.

POLITICAL LIFE

Trinidad and Tobago became independent from Britain in 1962 and has a fully democratic government, with elections held every five years. It is a Republic within the Commonwealth, with a President as Head of State. Executive power lies with the Prime Minister and the Cabinet. The legislature consists of an elected House of Representatives and an appointed Senate. Tobago has a separate House of Assembly controlling the island's domestic affairs.

Note: Politics is a serious business on both islands, but especially in Trinidad where electioneering can often turn violent. Caution should be exercised if visiting during an election.

PLANT AND ANIMAL LIFE

No other islands in the Caribbean can equal Trinidad and Tobago for the diversity of plant and wildlife. There are 433 different species of birds recorded on Trinidad and Tobago, 620 species of butterflies, 2,300 different flowering shrubs and plants, including 700 kinds of orchids. There are also 100 different species of mammals, including many species of bats, 70 species of reptiles and 25 species of amphibians.

Above: Cathedral, Port of Spain, Trinidad

Right: Botanic Gardens, Port of Spain, Trinidad

Trinidad and Tobago rank among the top ten countries in the world for the number of bird species per square mile, and many are South American species not found elsewhere in the Caribbean. The islands are also a major crossing point on the migration paths.

Because of the islands' proximity to South America and similar ecology, it uniquely not only boasts vegetation found on the mainland, but also on the other Caribbean islands.

Vegetation zones on the islands are clearly marked with highest areas displaying lush montane tropical rain forests with elfin woodlands close to the mountain summits. There are lowland rain forests, cultivated estates and small settlements which have been established in clearings on the hillside, and in the dry season, the hills are blanketed with the striking orange flowers of the mountain immortelle, a mountain tree that grows up to 80ft (24m) high, and the purple, yellow and golden blooms of the poui. Sugar cane is Trinidad's main crop and grown widely on the central plain, and there are fresh and salt water marshes, mangrove swamps and beach habitats.

There are palms of all descriptions, giant ferns and bamboos, almond, banyan, bananas, coconut groves, hanging breadfruit, mango, nutmeg, cocoa and pawpaw, and the most stunning array of spectacularly hued flowering plants from giant African tulip trees festooned with scarlet blossom to rare, tiny orchids. The island's teak is of the highest quality and much sought after. Bougainvillea flowers everywhere, there are scores of varieties of hibiscus, frangipani and poinsettia. There are heliconia, also known as the lobster

plant, bird of paradise flowers and anthurium everywhere. The flamboyant tree is also known as the tourist tree bursting into vivid bloom during the summer. It is called the tourist tree because it flowers in the summer and quickly turns red!

Along the coast you can find swamps, mangroves and marsh woodlands, while inland there are breathtaking walks through the high tropical rain forests. Beach morning glory with its array of pink flowers is found on many beaches, and is important because its roots help prevent sand drift. The plant also produces nectar from glands in the base of its leaf stalks that attract ants, and it is thought this evolution has occurred so that the ants will discourage any leaf-nibbling predators. Other beach plants include seagrape and the manchineel, which should be treated with caution.

Note: The manchineel, which can be found on many beaches, has a number of effective defensive mechanisms that can prove very painful. Trees vary from a few feet to more than 30 feet in height, and have widely spreading, deep forked boughs with small, dark green leaves and yellow stems, and fruit like small, green apples. If you examine the leaves carefully without touching them, you will notice a small pinhead sized raised dot at the junction of leaf and leaf stalk. The apple-like fruit is poisonous, and sap from the tree causes painful blisters. It is so toxic, that early Caribs are said to have dipped their arrowheads in it before hunting trips. Sap is released if a leaf or branch is broken, and more so after rain. Avoid contact with the tree, don't sit under it, or on a fallen branch, and do not eat the fruit. If you do get sap on your skin, run into the sea and wash it off as quickly as possible.

Of course, the sea teems with brilliantly hued fish and often, even more spectacularly tinted coral and marine plants. Even if you just float upside down in the water with a facemask on, you will be able to enjoy many of the beautiful underwater scenes, but the best way to see things is by scuba diving, snorkeling or taking a trip in a glass-bottomed boat.

Marine life abounds because the great Orinoco River floods into the Atlantic not far south of Trinidad. The nutrient-rich waters support a diversity of marine life much greater and more diverse than found elsewhere in the Caribbean.

There are scores of different corals that make up the reefs offshore, especially off Tobago. There are hard and soft corals and only one, the fire coral poses a threat to swimmers and divers, because if touched, it causes a stinging skin rash. Among the more spectacular corals are deadman's fingers, staghorn, brain coral and seafans, and there are huge sea anemones and sponges, while tropical fish species include the parrotfish, blue tang surgeonfish, tiny but aggressive damselfish, angelfish and brightly hued wrasse. You can swim with the manta rays, watch sharks and dolphins and observe the gentle manatee, or sea cow, especially off the south east of Trinidad.

Swamps also provide a rich habitat for wildlife. Tiny tree crabs and burrowing edible land crabs scurry around in the mud trapped in the roots of mangrove trees just above water level. Heron, egret, ibis, and pelican roost in the higher branches,

the mangrove cuckoo shares the lower branches with belted kingfishers. Offshore you can usually spot magnificent frigate birds.

Glorious gardens

Inland, gardens are generally ablaze with flowers in bloom all year round, growing alongside exotic vegetables like yam, sweet potato, and dasheen. Flowering plants include the flamboyant tree with their brilliant red flowers and dark brown seed pods, up to two feet long which can be used as rattles when the seeds have dried out inside. Bougainvillea grows everywhere and seems to be in bloom year round in a host of different shades. In fact, the shades do not come from petals but the plant's bract-like leaves which surround the small petal-less flowers. There are yellow and purple allamandas, amaryllis, chaconia, poinsettia, hibiscus, heliconia, giant anthurium, frangipani and bright flowers of the ixora.

The leaves of the travelers palm spread out like a giant open fan, and the tree got its name because the fan was believed to point from south to north, but it rarely does.

The flowers attract hummingbirds like the doctorbird, as well as

Continued on page 24...

21

Both islands offer countless opportunities for watching nature at close quarters, whether on land or below the sea. You can see giant leatherback turtles weighing more than 1,000lbs (454kg) hauling themselves up the beaches such as Matura, to lay their eggs in the sand. You can watch the huge colony of oilbirds emerge from the depths of the limestone caves of the Northern Range at dusk, or you can explore one of the world's richest marine environments off the coast of Tobago.

The brackish **Caroni Mangrove Swamp** is an important bird area, and the **Caroni Bird Sanctuary** is home to 130 species of birds including pelican, spoonbill, flamingo, egret and scarlet ibis – the national bird. The sight of hundreds of scarlet ibis flocking home to roost is one you will never forget.

The **Asa Wright Nature Centre and Lodge** is a must if you are at all interested in nature and wildlife. It is a world-famous 200-acre (80 hectare) conservation and research facility, 1,200ft (366m) up in the rainforests of the Northern Range mountains. It offers

guided nature walks and has 24 guest rooms and restaurant, and even during a pre-breakfast stroll you can spot up to 30 species of birds including the exotically named violaceous pepperstrike, turquoise-billed toucan, chestnut woodpecker, white-bearded manakin, bearded bellbird and rufus-browed pepperstrike. And, perhaps best of all, you can do your bird watching in style while sitting on the veranda of the old estate house and sipping a cool drink. There are guided walks along the nature trails at 10am and 1.30pm, and the facility is open daily from 9am to 5pm ☎667-4655.

The **Point-a-Pierre Wild Fowl Trust** is in the grounds of the oil refinery and breeds endangered birds and waterfowl for return to the wild. It has trails and a learning area, but it is advisable to phone first for visiting details ☎ 637-5145.

Other major nature attractions include the fresh water **Nariva Swamp**, one of the best places to spot red howler monkeys, manatee, alligators, anaconda, the rare Suriname toad and paradox frog, as well as many species of birds, including parrots and macaws. You might also see the unusual four eyed fish. There are 13 designated wildlife sanctuaries on Trinidad. There are the caves of **Mount Tamana**, the home of sightless, fish eating bats; the summit of **El Tucuche**, the domain of the unique golden tree frog, and **Saut d'Eau**, Trinidad's only pelican breeding ground. The **Aripo Savannahs** are noted for their wild flowers, including ancient species such as bladderwort and sundew, as well as unique ground orchids.

On Tobago, the **rainforests of the Main Ridge** were declared a protected area in 1764, the first to be established in the western hemisphere, and the area is still a sanctuary for an amazing variety of plant and wildlife species. Other eco-areas worth visiting are **Buccoo Reef** and **Nylon Pool**, the grounds of **the Arnos Vale Hotel**, the **Grafton Caledonia Wildlife Sanctuary**, the **Adventure Farm and Nature Reserve**, the **Botanical Gardens of Scarborough**, the **Louis d'Or Nurseries** near Roxborough, and the wetlands of **Bon Accord lagoon**, as well as the offshore islands of **Little Tobago** and **St Giles**, both important seabird sanctuaries.

the carib grackle, a strutting, starling-like bird with a paddle-shaped tail, and the friendly bananaquit. You can also spot tree lizards, and the larger geckos that hunt at night.

Along roadsides and hedgerows in the countryside, you can see the vine-like caralita, calabash with its gourd-like fruits, tamarind and distinctive star-shaped leaves of the castor bean, whose seeds when crushed yield castor oil.

And, areas of scrubland have their own flora or fauna, with plants bursting into flower following the first heavy rains after the dry season. There are century plants, with their prickly, sword like leaves, which grow for up to twenty years before flowering. The yellow flower stalk grows at a tremendous rate for several days and can reach 20ft (6m) high, but having bloomed once, the whole plant then dies. Other typical scrubland vegetation includes aloe, acacia, prickly pear and several species of cactus. Fiddlewood provides hard timber for furniture, bright and variegated crotons, the white flowered, aromatic frangipani and sea-island cotton, which used to provide the very finest cotton. Scrub vegetation also plays host to birds such as the mockingbird, ground dove, kingbird and grassquit, and it is the ideal habitat for lizards.

The rainforests provide the most prolific vegetation with mahogany trees, teaks, magnificent swathes of giant ferns, towering bamboo groves, enormous air plants, and a host of flowering or variegated plants such as heliconia, philodendron and wild fuchsia. There are balsa wood trees, the world's lightest wood, the flowering vine marcgravia, and the prolific mountain cabbage palm, and among the foliage and flowers you can find hummingbirds and parrots.

The forests are rich with small game that is hunted, especially the paca (known as the lappe), agouti, manicou (opossum), deer, collared peccary, tayra (wild dog) and quenk (peccary or wild hog.). The manicou lives in trees and forages over huge areas at night, and is not averse to rooting through trashcans for any delicacies. There is also the ocelot or tiger cat, anteater tatoo (armadillo), porcupine, iguana, crocodile and caiman, which is related to the alligator. And high in the trees you can see and hear capuchin and howler monkeys.

There are frogs and toads that croak loudly all night, lizards and snakes including the small but poisonous fer-de-lance. Plantation owners are said to have introduced the fer-de-lance to Trinidad. Ditches were dug round the slave quarters and filled with the snakes to discourage escape. The slaves may not have escaped but the snakes did and mongoose had to be introduced to keep the snakes under control. It is more likely, however, that the mongoose was introduced to control the snakes and rats in the sugar cane fields. There are fewer snakes on Tobago and all are non-poisonous.

Among the many species of freshwater fish is the guppy, first identified and named in Trinidad more than a century ago, and the cascadura, which according to legend has mystical powers. It is said that once you have eaten the fish, you will return to Trinidad to end your days.

Sea turtles

Lumbering sea turtles also come ashore at night between March and September to dig their shell nests in the sand and lay between 80 and 125 eggs. There are lots of opportunities to watch these endangered creatures but they should never be disturbed. The best turtle watching spots are on the leeward side of Tobago, and the north and east coasts of Trinidad, between the hours of 7pm and 5am. A turtle may nest six times at nine-day intervals on one season, laying more than 700 eggs. The incubation period ranges between fifty-five and seventy days and results in another incredible sight as the tiny, young hatchlings dash to the sea. The best time to see nesting leatherbacks is between June and July, with the hatchlings emerging between July and early October. Most nesting sites have guides who collect data on the turtles and lead the turtle watching groups.

There are butterflies, including the spectacular Blue Emperor, and less attractive insects such as mosquitoes, ants and sand flies.

There is also a remarkably rich and bright native bird life, including parrots and macaws, tropicbirds, toucans, ibis and spoon-bill, 17 species of hummingbirds, 15 species of egret, bittern and heron, three species of vulture, 24 species of falcon, hawk and harrier, plus owl, oilbird, goatsuckers, trogon, motmot, kingfishers, woodpeckers, woodcreepers, antbirds, flycatchers, manakins, mockingbird, vireos, warblers, honeycreepers, tanagers, grosbeaks and buntings and orioles.

Offshore you may sight the magnificent frigatebird, easily recognizable by its size, long black 7ft (2m)wing span, forked tail and apparent effortless ability to glide on the winds. There are brown booby birds, named by sailors from the Spanish word for 'fool' because they were so easy to catch. Pelicans that look so ungainly on land yet are so acrobatic in the air, are common, as are laughing gulls and royal terns. Several species of sandpiper can usually be seen scurrying around at the water's edge.

If you are really interested in bird watching pack a small pair of binoculars. The new mini-binoculars are ideal for island bird watching, because the light is normally so good that you will get a clear image despite the small object lens.

LOCAL PRODUCE

As most of the plants, fruits, vegetables and spices will be new to the first time visitor, the following brief descriptions are offered:

Bananas

Bananas have been such an important crop in the Caribbean they have earned the nickname 'green gold' – and they grow everywhere. There are three types of banana. The bananas that we normally buy in supermarkets originated in Malaya and were introduced into the Caribbean in the early sixteenth century by the Spanish. The large bananas, or plantains, originally came from southern India, and are largely used in cooking. They are often fried and served as an accompaniment to fish and meat. The third variety is the red banana, which is not grown commercially, but which can be seen around the island. Most banana plantations cover only a few acres and are worked by the owner or tenant, although there are still some very large holdings. A banana plant produces a crop about every nine months, and each cluster of flowers grows into a hand of bananas. A bunch can contain up to twenty hands of bananas, with each hand having up to twenty individual fruit.

Although they grow tall, bananas are not trees but herbaceous plants which die back each year. Once the plant has produced fruit, a shoot from the ground is cultivated to take its place, and the old plant dies. Bananas need a lot of attention, and island farmers will tell you that there are not enough hours in a day to do everything that needs to be done. The crop needs fertilizing regularly, leaves need cutting back, and you will often see the fruit inside blue tinted plastic containers, which protect it from insect and bird attack, and speeds up maturation.

Breadfruit

Breadfruit was introduced to the Caribbean in 1793 by Captain Bligh. He brought 1200 breadfruit saplings from Tahiti aboard the Providence, and these were first planted in Jamaica and St Vincent, and then quickly spread throughout the islands. It was Bligh's attempts to bring in young breadfruit trees that led to the mutiny on the *Bounty* four years earlier.

Mutiny on the Bounty

Bligh was given the command of the 215-ton *Bounty* in 1787 and was ordered to take the breadfruit trees from Tahiti to the West Indies where they were to be used to provide cheap food for the slaves. The ship had collected its cargo and had reached Tonga when the crew, under Fletcher Christian, mutinied. The crew claimed that Bligh's regime was too tyrannical, and he and eighteen members of the crew who stayed loyal to him, were cast adrift in an open boat. The cargo of breadfruit was dumped overboard. Bligh, in a remarkable feat of seamanship, navigated the boat for 3,600 miles until making landfall on Timor in the East Indies. Some authorities have claimed that it was the breadfruit tree cargo that sparked the mutiny, as each morning the hundreds of trees in their heavy containers had to be carried on deck, and then carried down into the hold at nightfall. It might have proved just too much for the already overworked crew.

Whatever the reason for the mutiny, the breadfruit is a cheap carbohydrate-rich food, although pretty tasteless when boiled. It is

Above: Mangoes

Right: Breadfruit

Below: Tropical forest at the Asa Wright Nature Centre, Trinidad

best eaten fried, baked or roasted over charcoal. The slaves did not like it at first, but the tree spread and now can be found almost everywhere. It has large dark, green leaves, and the large green fruits can weigh 10-12lbs (about 5kg). The falling fruits explode with a loud bang and splatter their pulpy contents over a large distance. It is said that no one goes hungry when the breadfruit is in season.

Calabash

Calabash trees are native to the Caribbean and have huge gourd-like fruits that are very versatile when dried and cleaned. They can be used as water containers and bowls, bailers for boats, and as lanterns. Juice from the pulp is boiled into a syrup and used to treat coughs and colds, and the fruit is said to have many other medicinal uses.

RECIPE FOR TOBAGO CURRY CRAB AND DUMPLINGS

You need:

- 2 large cooked crabs
- 3 cups of coconut milk
- 1 large onion
- chives
- stick of celery
- 2 tablespoons curry powder
- 2 tablespoons of cooking oil
- salt to taste

Season the crabmeat with salt, chop the celery into cubes and finely chop the chives and half the onion. Brown the curry powder in the oil in a pan and sate the rest of the sliced onion. Add the coconut milk and crab to the pan and cook for 20 to 25 minutes. Serve with the dumplings.

For dumplings you need:

- 4 cups of flour
- half a cup of water
- 2 tablespoons of butter
- salt to taste

Mix the ingredients and add water till all the flour has been absorbed. Place in a covered dish and leave to stand for 5 to 10 minutes. Then knead thoroughly until the dough is smooth. Cut the dough into sections and shape into small balls which when rolled flat are about half an inch thick. Cook in boiling water for about 10 minutes.

Cocoa

Cocoa is another important crop, and its Latin name *theobroma* means 'food of the gods'. A cocoa tree can produce several thousand flowers a year, but only a fraction of these will develop into seed bearing pods. It is the heavy orange pods that hang from the cocoa tree which contain the beans that contain the seeds that produce cocoa and chocolate. The beans, containing a sweet, white sap that protects the seeds, are split open and kept in trays to ferment. This process takes up to eight days and the seeds must be kept at a regular temperature to ensure the right taste and aroma develop. The seeds are then dried. In the old days people used to walk barefoot over the beans to polish them to enhance their appearance. Today, the beans are crushed to extract cocoa butter, and the remaining powder is cocoa.

Chocolate drink

You can sometimes buy cocoa balls in the markets which make a delicious drink. Each ball is the size of a large cherry. For a rich chocolate drink, simply dissolve the ball in a pan of boiling water, simmer, add sugar, milk or cream, Each ball will make about four delicious mugs of chocolate.

Coconut

Coconut palms are everywhere and should be treated with caution. Anyone who has heard the whoosh of a descending coconut knows how scary the sound is. Those who did not hear the whoosh, presumably did not live to tell the tale. It is not a good idea to picnic in a coconut grove!

Coconut trees are incredibly hardy, able to grow in sand and even when regularly washed by salty seawater. They can also survive long periods without rain. Their huge leaves, up to 20ft (6m) long in mature trees, drop down during dry spells so a smaller surface area is exposed to the sun, reducing evaporation. Coconut palms can grow up to 80ft (24m) tall, and produce up to 100 seeds a year. The seeds are the second largest in the plant kingdom, and these fall when ripe.

The coconut traditionally bought in greengrocers is the seed surrounded by a hard shell. In its natural state this is then covered by copra, a fibrous material, and enclosed in a large green husk. The seed and protective coverings can weigh 30lbs (13.6kg) and more. The seed and casing is waterproof, drought proof and able to float, and this explains why coconut palms which originated in the Pacific and Indian Oceans, are now found throughout the Caribbean – the seeds literally floated across the seas.

The coconut palm is extremely versatile. The leaves can be used as thatch for roofing, or cut into strips and woven into matting and baskets, while the husks yield coir, which is resistant to salt water and ideal for ropes and brushes and brooms. Green coconuts contain delicious thirst-quenching 'milk', and the coconut 'meat' can be eaten raw, or baked in ovens for two days before being sent to processing plants where the oil is extracted.

Coconut oil is used in cooking, soaps, synthetic rubber, and even in hydraulic brake fluid.

As you travel around the islands, you will see groups of men and women splitting the coconuts in half with machetes. You might also see halved coconut shells spaced out on the corrugated tin roofs of some homes. These are being dried before being sold to the copra processing plants.

Dasheen

Dasheen is one of the crops known as 'ground provisions' in the islands, the others being potatoes, yams, eddo and tannia. The last two are close relatives of dasheen, and all are members of the aroid family, some of the world's oldest cultivated crops. Dasheen with its 'elephant ear' leaves, and eddo grow from a corm which when boiled thoroughly can be used like potato, and the young leaves of either are used to make callaloo, a spinach-like soup. Both dasheen and eddo are thought to have come from China or Japan but tannia is native to the Caribbean, and its roots can be boiled, baked or fried.

Guava

Guava has an aromatic, pulpy fruit that is also enjoyed by birds who then distribute its seeds. The fruit is used to make a wide range of products from jelly to 'cheese', a paste made by mixing the fruit with sugar. The fruit varies from a golf ball to a tennis ball in size, is a rich source of vitamin A and contains much more vitamin C than citrus fruit.

Opposite page: Selling green coconut's to drink, Tobago

Mango

Mango can be delicious if somewhat messy to eat. It originally came from India but is now grown throughout the Caribbean and found wherever there are people. Young mangoes can be stringy and unappetizing, but ripe fruit from mature trees that grow up to 50ft (15m) and more, are usually delicious, and can be eaten raw or cooked. The juice is a great reviver in the morning, and the fruit is often used to make jams and other preserves. The wood of the mango is often used by boatbuilders.

Nutmeg

Nutmeg trees are sometimes found. The tree thrives in hilly, wet areas and the fruit is the size of a small tomato. The outer husk, which splits open while still on the tree, is used to make the very popular nutmeg jelly. Inside, the seed is protected by a bright red casing that when dried and crushed, produces the spice mace. Finally, the dark outer shell of the seed is broken open to reveal the nutmeg which is dried and then ground into a powder, or sold whole so that it can be grated to add spice to dishes.

Passion fruit

Passion fruit is not widely grown but it can be bought at the market. The pulpy fruit contains hundreds of tiny seeds, and many people prefer to press the fruit and drink the juice. It is also commonly used in fruit salads, sherbets and ice creams.

Pawpaw

Pawpaw trees are also found throughout the islands and are commonly grown in gardens. The trees are prolific fruit producers but grow so quickly that the fruit soon becomes difficult to gather. The large, juicy, melon-like fruits are eaten fresh, pulped for juice or used locally to make jams, preserves and ice cream. They are rich sources of vitamin A and C. The leaves and fruit contain an enzyme which tenderizes meat, and tough joints cooked wrapped in pawpaw leaves or covered in slices of fruit, usually taste like much more expensive cuts. The same enzyme, papain, is also used in chewing gum, cosmetics, the tanning industry and, somehow, in making wool shrink resistant. A tea made from unripe fruit is said to be good for lowering high blood pressure.

Pigeon Peas

Pigeon Peas are cultivated and can often be found in back gardens. The plants are very hardy and drought resistant, and are prolific yielders of peas that can be eaten fresh or dried and used in soups and stews.

Pineapples

Pineapples were certainly grown in the Caribbean by the time Columbus arrived, and were probably brought from South America by the Amerindians. The fruit is slightly smaller than the Pacific pineapple, but the taste more intense.

Sugar cane

Sugar cane can still be seen growing. The canes can grow up to 12ft (3.7m) tall and when cut have to be crushed to extract the sugary juice. Most estates had their own sugar mill powered by waterwheels or windmills. The remains of many of these mills can still be seen around the island, and much of the original machinery, mostly made in Britain,

is still in place. After extraction, the juice was boiled until the sugar crystallized. The mixture remaining was molasses and this was used to produce rum.

Sugar apple

Sugar apple is a member of the annona fruit family, and grows wild and in gardens throughout the islands. The small, soft, sugar apple fruit can be peeled off in strips when ripe, and is like eating thick applesauce. They are eaten fresh or used to make sherbet or drinks. Soursop, is a member of the same family, and its spiny fruits can be seen in hedgerows and gardens. They are eaten fresh or used for preserves, drinks and ice cream.

FOOD AND DRINK

Dining out in the Caribbean offers the chance to experiment with all sorts of unusual spices, exotic vegetables and fruits, with the freshest of seafood, Creole and island dishes, and, of course, rum punches and other exotic cocktails. And, because of its diverse population, the cuisine of Trinidad and Tobago is even more exciting with East Indian, Chinese, Creole, Italian, Lebanese and Latin American influences. There are also fast food outlets serving both American burgers and fried chicken, and traditional Trinidadian fast food snacks.

Many hotels have a tendency to offer buffet dinners or barbecues, but even these can be interesting and tasty affairs. Eating out is generally very relaxed, and few restaurants have a strict dress code, although most people like to wear something a little smarter at dinner after a day on the beach or out sightseeing.

BREAKFASTS

These can be very healthy with wonderful exotic fruit juices and fresh fruit. There is watermelon, mango, pineapple, bananas and papaya. Local breakfast dishes include fish buljol, tomato choka, fried accra and tannia cakes.

You could also try doubles – curried chickpeas, ladled onto lightly fried dough – for a different start of the day meal. You will see scores of doubles vendors on the streets and most locals insist their supplier serves the best doubles on the island. Black pudding is popular, a legacy of both English and French ancestry, while souse is another traditional dish consisting of cold boiled pork served in a piquant sauce with slices of cucumber, lime, pepper and onion.

LUNCHES

These are best eaten at beach cafés that usually offer excellent barbecued fresh fish and conch – which often appears on menus as lambi (not to be confused with lamb). Lobster and crab is also widely available, especially on Tobago where one of the national dishes is crab and dumplings. Dishes are mostly served with local vegetables such as fried plantain, cassava and yam, and fresh fruit such as pineapple, mango, golden apple or papaya, makes an ideal and light dessert.

DINNER

There is an enormous choice when it comes to dinner. Starters include traditional Caribbean dishes such as christophene and coconut soup, and Callaloo soup made from the leaves of dasheen, a spinach like vegetable also called elephant's ears, with okra, pumpkin and coconut milk added. On special occasions crab or other meats are added. Fish and clam chowders are also popular starters. Try heart of palm, excellent fresh shrimps or scallops, smoked kingfish wrapped in crêpes or crab backs, succulent land crab meat sautéed with breadcrumbs and seasoning, and served stuffed back in the shell. It is much sweeter than the meat of sea crabs. On Tobago, curried crab and dumpling is a specialty.

The fish is generally excellent, and do not be alarmed if you see dolphin on the menu. It is not the protected species made famous by 'Flipper', but a solid, close-textured flat-faced fish called dorado, which is delicious. There are also tuna, snapper, lobster, swordfish, baby squid and mussels, and Tobago is noted for its flying fish, delicious when fried. Try buljol which is shredded saltfish served with tomatoes, onions, peppers, avocado and olive oil.

Try seafood jambalaya, chunks of lobster, shrimps and ham served on a bed of braised seasoned rice, shrimp Creole, with fresh shrimp sautéed in garlic butter and parsley and served with tomatoes, or fish Creole, with fresh fish steaks cooked in a spicy onion, garlic and tomato sauce and served with rice and fried plaintain. Other island dishes include sautéed scallops with ginger, curried fish steaks lightly fried with a curry sauce and served with sliced bananas, cucumber, fresh coconut and rice.

Pelau reflects the Creole influence and is slow stewed beef or chicken cooked with brown rice and pigeon peas. Be careful, however, as it can often be spiced up with peppers. Chickpeas, also called chana, are regularly served, and dahl is dried split peas cooked in soup or with rice, while pholouri (or phulori) are fritters made with split peas. Other Creole dishes include stewed chicken and fried fish served with a variety of vegetables such as boiled cassava, roast breadfruit, fried plantain, yam and eddoes.

It seems such a waste to travel to the Caribbean and eat burgers and steaks, especially when there are many much more exciting meat dishes available.

The East Indian influence is represented by curry and roti, Trinidadian fast food with a difference. It is an envelope of paper-thin soft split pea dough containing rich curry and vegetables. You can get different fillings – beef, pork, chicken and fish as well as combinations – and if you get the chance, try the chicken, pumpkin and channa combo. The chicken roti can contain bones that some people like

to chew on, so be warned. There is also aloo pie made from potatoes. Another East Indian influence is the general use of words such as bhag for spinach, and baigan for eggplant.

You could try curried chicken, goat and fish sometimes served in a coconut shell, gingered chicken with mango and spices; Caribbean souse, with cuts of lean pork marinated with shredded cucumber, onions, garlic, lime juice and pepper sauce.

For vegetarians there are excellent salads, stuffed breadfruit, breadfruit pie, callaloo bake, stuffed squash and pawpaw, baked sweet potato and yam casserole.

For dessert, try fresh fruit salad, or one of the exotic tasting home-made ice creams, like mango or coconut. There are banana fritters and banana flambé, coconut cheesecake and tropical fruit sorbets, or try bene balls, sugary balls coated with sesame seeds.

FOOD ADVICE

Most menus and dishes are self explanatory, but one or two things are worth bearing in mind. When green fig appears on the menu, it usually means green banana, which is peeled and boiled as a vegetable. It is often served with salt fish that used to be salted cod, but now it can be any fish. On the buffet table, you will often see a dish called pepper pot. This is usually hot, spicy meat and vegetable stew to which may be added small flour dumplings and shrimps.

There are wonderful breads in the Caribbean, and you should try them if you get the chance. There are banana and pumpkin breads, and delicious cakes such as coconut loaf cake, guava jelly cookies and rum cake.

Above: Bird watchers on Caroni Swamp, Trinidad
Below: Port of Spain, Trinidad
Opposite page: Old Powder House, Tobago

Don't be afraid to eat out. Food is often prepared in front of you, and there are some great snacks, both savory and sweet, available from island eateries. Most of the stalls are run by women, who cook in the open air. Try roti, deep fried cakes of dough called floats, or saltfish or corned beef fritters. You can buy pastels, balls of beef, peppers and raisins, which are traditionally wrapped in dasheen leaves. For sweet snacks try coconut patties called pamies, or bene balls made from sesame. As you drive around, there is no shortage of stalls selling fresh fruit, all of which make a refreshing and healthy meal.

Another note of warning: on most tables you will find a bottle of pepper sauce. It usually contains a blend of several types of hot pepper, spices and vinegar, and should be treated cautiously. Try a little first before splashing it all over your food, as these sauces range from hot to unbearable.

Home-made sauce

If you want to make your own hot pepper sauce, take four ripe hot peppers, one teaspoon each of oil, ketchup and vinegar and a pinch of salt, blend together into a liquid, and bottle.

There are a number of specialty foods which are only prepared during special religious festivals. Pastelles, is from an ancient traditional Spanish recipe, and contains seasoned mincemeat wrapped in corn meal dough. It only appears at Christmas time and can contain all sorts of other ingredients such as olives, capers and raisins. The pastelles are wrapped in banana leaves for easy transport.

DRINKS

Rum is the Caribbean drink. There are almost as many rums in the West Indies as there are malt whiskies in Scotland, and there is an amazing variety of strength, shade and quality. The first West Indian rum was produced in the Danish Virgin Islands in the 1660s and by the end of the century there were thousands of distilleries throughout the Caribbean. Rum rapidly became an important commodity and figured prominently in the infamous Triangle Trade in which slaves from Africa were sold for rum in the West Indies, which was then sold to raise money to buy more slaves.

Rum has such fortifying powers that General George Washington insisted every soldier be given a daily tot, and a daily ration also became a tradition in the British Royal Navy, one that lasted from the eighteenth century until 1970.

Columbus is credited with planting the first sugar cane in the Caribbean, on Hispaniola, during his third voyage, and the Spanish called the drink produced from it aguardiente de cane, although it was officially named as saccharum, from the Latin name for sugar cane. It was English sailors who abbreviated this name to rum. It is sometimes suggested that the word rum comes from an abbreviation of the word 'rumbullion'. While the origin of this word is unknown there is a record of it in 1672, and it was later used to describe a drunken brawl.

Rum can be produced in two ways. It can be distilled directly from the fermented juice of crushed sugar cane, or made from molasses left after sugar, extracted from the cane by crushing, is boiled until it crystallizes. Dark rums need extensive ageing in oak barrels, sometimes for up to fifteen years, while light rums are more light-bodied and require less ageing.

Mix Your Own

The Painkiller is a rum cocktail containing orange and pineapple juice, cream of coconut and a sprinkling of nutmeg. There are scores of different rum cocktails, and one of the most popular is the traditional Caribbean Plantation Rum Punch.

To make **Plantation Rum Punch**, thoroughly mix 3 ounces of rum, with one ounce of limejuice and one teaspoon of honey, then pour over crushed ice, and for a little zest, add a pinch of freshly grated nutmeg.

Planter's Punch: combine 2 ounces each of pineapple juice, rum, cream of coconut and half an ounce of lime in a blender for one minute. Pour into a chilled glass, add a sprinkle of grated coconut and garnish with a slice of cherry and a slice of orange.

Most of the production is of white rum, and there are some excellent barrel-aged drinks that are best sipped and enjoyed as liqueurs.

Most tourist hotels and bars also offer a wide range of cocktails both alcoholic, usually very strong, and non-alcoholic. Tap water in hotels and resorts is generally safe to drink and mineral and bottled water is widely available, and so are soft drinks. There is good island beer, especially the excellent Carib, and a huge choice of fruit juices and home made drinks like ginger beer, and shandies made with sorrel and mauby and a little beer. Green coconuts with the top sliced off to make a drinking hole, provide a very refreshing and cheap drink, and an experience worthy of a souvenir photo.

Take it easy

Note: While many of the main tourist hotel restaurants offer excellent service, time does not have the same urgency as it does back home, and why should it after all, as you are on holiday. Relax, enjoy a drink, the company and the surroundings and don't worry if things take longer, the wait is generally worth it.

Trinidad

Port of Spain is a bustling, pulsating, crowded cosmopolitan city that is a mix of traditional and modern, with delightful, pastel hued gingerbread houses and nineteenth century cathedrals contrasting with the high rise office blocks and busy port. It has magnificent old buildings, manicured, elegant suburbs, wonderful wide-open spaces and lively nightspots. The 'Trinis' love to party or 'fete', and there is no shortage of opportunities to do so from sophisticated clubs to earthy soca bars which never seem to close. There are historic buildings such as the splendid Whitehall, the imposing Edwardian School and the Gothic Scottish-style Stollmeyer's Castle, and it is an easy city to explore because it is laid out in grid-style with most streets running parallel or at right angles to each other. Port of Spain became the island capital in 1757 and grew rapidly but was virtually burned to the ground by fire in 1808. Governor Woodford then set about planning a new town from scratch, the results of which can still be seen today.

EXPLORING THE CITY

Downtown, between Independence Square, and the Queen's Park Savannah, is a constant clamor with busy streets, traffic jammed roads and goods of all sorts spilling out of the stores on to the sidewalks. There are street vendors offering everything from nuts and tasty snacks to arts and crafts goods, rolls of cloth to music cassettes; alleys packed with intriguing shops and modern shopping malls.

Independence Square is not a square at all, but a large rectangle made up of several squares and running parallel with the sea and inland from Queen's Wharf. Around the square with its patterned red brickwork are banks and modern government buildings, stores, fast food outlets and theatres. To the east of the square is the Roman Catholic Cathedral, with the imposing Twin Towers of the city's financial complex to the west, but the square itself offers an oasis with trees and benches, chess tables and the new **Brian Lara Promenade**, named after Trinidad's cricket hero.

The **Cathedral of the Immaculate Conception** stands on the eastern side of Independence Square, and it is interesting because when it was completed in 1832 it was on the waterfront. All the land now standing between it and the sea has been reclaimed. The Roman Catholic cathedral is built of stone that was quarried from nearby Laventille. The cathedral is worth visiting for its stained glass windows and magnificent wooden ceiling, and after entering through the large wooden doors stop and look at the altar loft over them.

There are lots of streets to explore which run inland from Independence Square. There is the pink Globe Theatre on St. Vincent Street, and if you take Frederick Street there are two shopping malls and the People's Mall, which is a must. It is the focus for the capital's arts and crafts community, offering a wide range of goods, most of which make fine souvenirs. It can be a little intimidating in the People's Mall at first because it is so busy with lots of noise and action. You can buy woven goods, hand-made jewels and items crafted from wood, leather, shells and other natural materials.

Meeting place

Continue along Frederick Street and you come to **Woodford Square** (named after Governor Woodford), which has long been the venue for political and religious meetings. It is Trinidad's equivalent to Speaker's Corner in London's Hyde Park and there is even a blackboard for those who want to write down their views for others to read and comment on.

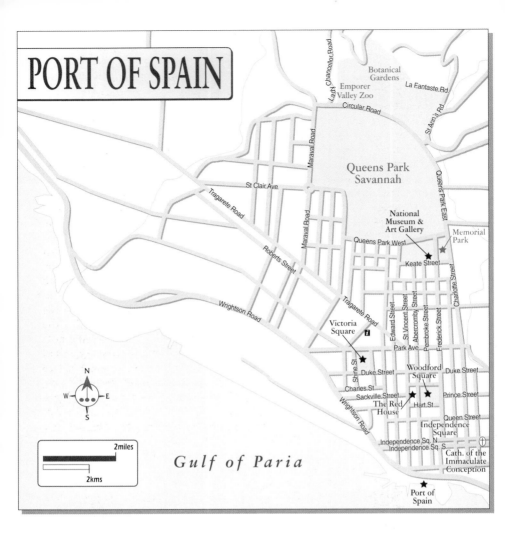

PORT OF SPAIN

Chancellor Road
Lady
Botanical
Gardens
Emporer
Valley Zoo
La Fantaste Rd
Circular Road
St Ann's Rd

Maraval Road

Queens Park
Savannah

St Clair Ave

Tragarete Road

Queen's Park East

National
Museum &
Art Gallery

Memorial
Park

Maraval Road

Queens Park West

Roberts Street

Keate Street

Charlotte Street

Wrightson Road

Tragarete Road

Victoria
Square

Edward Street
St Vincent Street
Abercromby Street
Pembroke Street
Frederick Street

Park Ave

Shine St.

Duke Street

Woodford
Square

Duke Street

N

W ─ E

S

Charles St.
Sackville Street
Wrightson Road
The Red
House
Hart St.

Prince Street

Queen Street
Independence
Square

2miles

Independence Sq. N.
Independence Sq. S.

Cath. of the
Immaculate
Conception

2kms

Gulf of Paria

Port of
Spain

Several grand old colonial buildings including the public library and Anglican Cathedral flank it. **Trinity Anglican Cathedral** is on the south side of the square, and was completed in 1818 although not consecrated until 1823. The roof, supported by mahogany beams, was copied from Westminster Hall in London. On the opposite side of the square is Abercromby Street and the **Red House**, the islands' parliament building. It was painted red in 1897 to mark the Diamond Jubilee of Queen Victoria. The building, which houses both chambers of parliament, can be visited and admission is free.

Continue north inland and you reach Port of Spain's heart, **Queen's Park Savannah**, a vast 200 acre (80 hectares) of greenery, trees, fine buildings, theatre and until recently, the island's premier race course. It is 2.5 miles (4km) around the perimeter of the Savannah and there is a paved path that is ideal for fitness walking and jogging. The joggers appear as early as 4am and hundreds of people exercise or just stroll around it in the early evening. It is also claimed that because the road around the Savannah is one way, it constitutes the world's largest traffic roundabout. The Savannah itself accommodates a wide range of sporting activities from the national game of cricket, to rugby, football and hockey. There are picnic areas and benches around a small pond at The Hollows, and if you haven't brought your own food, there are scores of stalls around the perimeter where you can buy green coconuts for a refreshing drink, roasted corn on the cob, all sorts of fruits and snacks from rotis to other Trinidadian fast foods, all cheap and tasty.

The Savannah contains Nobel Prize winner Derek Walcott's **Trinidad Theatre Workshop**, the **Spektakula Forum**, a shrine to calypso, and scores of shops, bars and restaurants. Among the most appealing sights are the beautifully behaved children in their immaculate uniforms heading to and from their downtown schools.

The Magnificent Seven

Another sight not to be missed is the **Magnificent Seven** – seven spectacular colonial mansions in a row along the north-west rim of the Savannah. All the grand houses were built at the beginning of this century by wealthy plantation owners, and it seems as if they were trying to outdo each other with architectural styles which range from the Queen's Royal College, the Scottish-style Gothic Stollmeyer Castle to a classical French chateau, and a Moorish-style mansion called the White House inspired by a Venetian-style palazzo, the Archbishop's Palace and the Gingerbread House.

The **Botanic Gardens** are on the northern side of the Savannah. The 62-acres (24.8 hectares) of grounds were laid out by Governor Woodford in 1818 with plants and trees from around the world, and the results were so pleasing to him, that he moved his official residence there. Among the many wonderful plants is the chaconia, the national flower of Trinidad and Tobago, and the incredible raw beef tree which bleeds if the bark is scratched but then heals itself. There are also many herbal, spice and fruit plants and you can smell the bark of the cinnamon, the leaves of aniseed and the delicate aroma of nutmeg. Visit the Orchid Display House and see how many of the 700 different species of trees, most of them indigenous to Trinidad and Tobago, you can spot. You will be approached by calypso singers and unofficial tour guides. Either politely tell them you are not interested or listen to a song and then have an interesting, if not always accurate, botanic tour in return for a reasonable tip.

The official homes of the President and the Prime Minister are on the right hand side of the Botanic Gardens, set in their own manicured grounds, and the **Emperor Valley Zoo** is on the left hand side. It is named after the emperor butterfly that was originally found there.

Memorial Park and the **National Museum** are at the south-east corner of the Savannah. The National Museum and Art Gallery features exhibits from the country's past and the national art collection, including paintings by Trinidad's nineteenth-century artist Michael Jean Cazabon.

Continued on page 44...

41

TRINIDAD

The Dragon's Mouth

Maqueripe Bay

La Vache Point
La Vache Bay
Maracas Bay
Morro Point
Balata Bay

Crozal Point

Water Park

North Coast Rd

Maracas Bay Village

Diego Martin
Petit Valley
Maraval
Santa Cruz

N
W E
S

Huevos

Boca Grande
Boca De Navios
Boca De Huevos

Monos
Chaguaramas

Fort George
St Ann s
Cascade

St James

Chacachacare

Boca De Monos

Gaspar Grande

St Peters Bay

St Joseph

Chaguaramas National Park

Fort St Andre

Barataria

Fort Chacon

Fort Picton

Port-of-Spain

Caroni Swamp Nat. Park

Uriah Butler Hwy

Chaguanas

Barracones Bay

Waterloo

Carapichaima

Couva
Couva

Cangrejos Bay

California
Lisas Bay

Claxton Bay

St Margaret

Solomon Hochoy Hwy

Point-a-Pierre Wildfowl Trust

Gasparille

Marabella
Vistabella

San Fernando

Mon Repos
Ste Madalein

The Pitch Lake

La Brea
Otaheite Bay

Canaan

South Trunk Rd

St Marys

Fyzabad

Debe

Guapo Bay

Point Fortin

Irois Bay

Guapo

Penal

Granville Bay

Irois

Granville

Southern Main Rd

Buenos Ayre

Los Bajos

Siparia

Columbus Bay

Bonasse

Chatham

Palo Seco

Morne Diablo

Fullarton

Islote Bay

Islote Point

Erin Bay

San Francique

Los Iros Bay

Erin Point

Palo Seco Bay

Roja Point

Quinam Bay

Icacos

0   5 miles

0   5Km

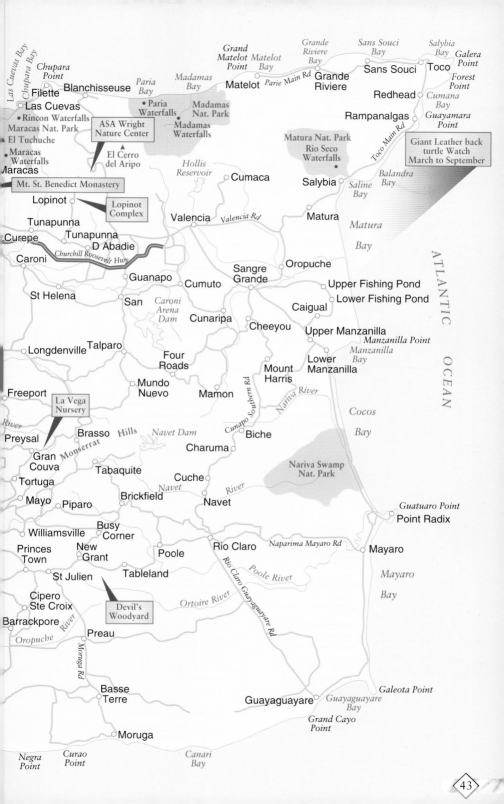

Las Cuevas Bay
Chupara Bay
Chupara Point
Filette
Blanchisseuse
Paria Bay
Las Cuevas
Rincon Waterfalls
Maracas Nat. Park
El Tuchuche
Maracas Waterfalls
Maracas
Paria Waterfalls
ASA Wright Nature Center
El Cerro del Aripo
Mt. St. Benedict Monastery
Lopinot
Lopinot Complex
Madamas Bay
Madamas Nat. Park
Madamas Waterfalls
Grand Matelot Point
Matelot Bay
Matelot
Parie Main Rd
Grande Riviere Bay
Sans Souci Bay
Sans Souci
Salybia Bay
Galera Point
Toco
Forest Point
Cumana Bay
Grande Riviere
Redhead
Rampanalgas
Guayamara Point
Toco Main Rd
Hollis Reservoir
Cumaca
Matura Nat. Park
Rio Seco Waterfalls
Salybia
Saline Bay
Balandra Bay
Giant Leather back turtle Watch March to September
Tunapunna
Curepe
Tunapunna
D Abadie
Caroni
Churchill Roosevelt Hwy
Valencia
Valencia Rd
Matura
Matura Bay
ATLANTIC OCEAN
St Helena
Guanapo
San
Caroni Arena Dam
Cumuto
Sangre Grande
Oropuche
Cunaripa
Cheeyou
Upper Fishing Pond
Lower Fishing Pond
Caigual
Upper Manzanilla
Manzanilla Point
Manzanilla Bay
Longdenville
Talparo
Four Roads
Mount Harris
Lower Manzanilla
Freeport
La Vega Nursery
Mundo Nuevo
Mamon
Cunapo Southern Rd
Nariwa River
Cocos Bay
River
Preysal
Brasso
Hills
Navet Dam
Biche
Gran Couva
Monserrat
Charuma
Nariva Swamp Nat. Park
Tabaquite
Cuche
Tortuga
Navet
River
Mayo
Piparo
Brickfield
Navet
Guatuaro Point
Point Radix
Williamsville
Busy Corner
Rio Claro
Naparima Mayaro Rd
Mayaro
Princes Town
New Grant
Poole
Rio Claro Guayaguayare Rd
Mayaro Bay
St Julien
Tableland
Poole River
Cipero
Ste Croix
Devil's Woodyard
Ortoire River
Barrackpore
River
Preau
Oropuche
Moruga Rd
Galeota Point
Basse Terre
Guayaguayare
Guayaguayare Bay
Moruga
Grand Cayo Point
Negra Point
Curao Point
Canari Bay

Port of Spain has a lively arts scene with a number of private galleries and several theatres offering productions from the serious to the avant-garde. Main theaters are: Little Carib Theater, Planteurs, Queen's Hall and the Space Theater.

Also worth visiting is the Angostura Distillery in the Fernandes Compound east of Port of Spain. It produces rum and the world-famous Angostura Bitters. There is an art gallery featuring the work of local artists. North of Port of Spain is the prosperous superb of Maraval with many good restaurants.

Nightspots include the very lively Club Coconuts, the Attic and Pelican Pub in Cascade. Or, you can just

GETTING AROUND TRINIDAD

There are daily air and ferry services between Trinidad and Tobago. Air Caribbean has several flights daily between the two islands and the crossing takes about 15 minutes. The sea ferry crossing takes 5 hours and can be choppy.

On Trinidad, the Government-run PTSC (Public Transport Service Corporation) operates buses along all the main island routes. It is a very cheap, efficient and fun way to travel, and the buses do generally run to schedule, but you have to buy your ticket at the bus station before boarding and the ticket office is usually closed early morning, in the evening and at weekends. Comfortable express buses (ECS for Express Commuter Services) run north to south between Port of Spain,

Shopping

Downtown Port of Spain offers a wide range of shopping, especially the large duty free stores on Frederick and Charlotte Streets which run from Independence Square. Leather goods, especially shoes and belts, are offered by Rastafarian craftsmen, who also create jewels in their small shops in the warren of back streets. Be prepared for banter and be ready to barter. There is great island music from steel pan to calypso and soca, and cassettes always make a good souvenir. The People's Mall always yields interesting traditional goods and souvenirs, while the capital's most popular shopping areas are Long Circular Mall in St. James and West Mall in Westmoorings.

enjoy the sunset from one of the many bars and restaurants along the front at St. James, or take in the view from Wazo Deyzeel, just north of the Savannah.

THE NORTH OF THE ISLAND

The north-west **Chaguaramas peninsula** is Trinidad's main tourist area and the indented coastline and many offshore islands provide safe and secluded anchorages which attract hundreds of yachts from around the world. Trinidad not only has near

Chaguanas, and San Fernando. The buses are air-conditioned and tickets can be purchased at PTSC South Quay bus terminal, and at Bhaggan's Drugs on Independence Square. Typical ECS fares are: Airport to Port of Spain TT$4, and Port of Spain to San Fernando and Port of Spain to Arima TT$6.For information call 623-7872.

Taxis, shared taxis and private mini buses (called maxi-taxis) have registration plates beginning with the letter 'H'. The public buses run from the Piarco airport to Port of Spain roughly every hour and cost TT$1.50.

Shared taxis and maxi-taxis also offer a cheap way to travel around, and for long distances between towns you can take an air-conditioned express bus. Maxi taxis used to be deafeningly loud with music playing full volume but the drivers have been ordered to turn their radios down. The maxi buses are still crowded but they are very cheap and a very good way of getting around and meeting the locals. They are marked with different stripes that indicate the areas in which they operate. Buses operating in and around Port of Spain have yellow stripes, those working around eastern Trinidad have red stripes, while green stripes indicate the south part of the island, black for Princes Town, and brown for San Fernando and the south-west. There are no fixed bus stops; you just flag down the bus as it approaches. Just before your destination shout 'stop' loud enough for the driver to hear you, otherwise you will go racing past where you want to get off, much to the amusement of your fellow passengers.

There are fixed taxi fares from Piarco International and Crown Point International Airports. It is about 16 miles (25km) from Piarco to Port of Spain and the fare is TT$120, to Maraval it is TT$164, and San Fernando TT$186, with surcharges after 10pm and before 6am. It is 8 miles (13km) from Crown Point to Scarborough and the fare is TT$54, to Speyside it is TT$216 and Charlotteville TT$240.

Some journeys do not have a fixed price and as the taxis are not metered, make sure you know what the cost will be before setting off.

perfect waters for cruising, but also all the facilities long-haul yachts need, both for repairs and re-stocking, and at prices well below those charged in more fashionable locations further north in the Caribbean. The island also makes a handy base for those wanting to cruise the Caribbean or for those wanting a break before heading further west through the Panama Canal into the Pacific. Many other yachts anchor here during the late summer and autumn to avoid the hurricane belt further north. For visitors staying in and around Port of Spain there is a lot to see and do in this bustling corner of the island.

Overlooking the capital and defending its sea approaches is **Fort George**. A few of the old buildings built by the British remain together with some cannon, but a visit is worthwhile because of the great views. The **River Estate Water Wheel** stands at the end of the Diego Martin valley north west of Port of Spain, and is a reminder of the island's historic dependence on sugar cane. The estate house has been restored and there is also a small museum. And, running off

Diego Martin Valley is Petit Valley where you can visit the **Blue Basin Waterfall**, a five-minute walk along a path from the road running north from Diego Martin village.

The 14,500-acre (5,800 hectares) Chaguaramas peninsula is the main focus for yachting in the area, with marinas and boatyards where repairs can be carried out. The peninsula used to be occupied by large estates growing sugar cane, coffee and cocoa, with isolated and small fishing villages scattered around the coast. During the World War II the peninsula was handed over to the United States Navy and became the home of a strategically important naval base protecting the southern approaches to the Caribbean. The base was handed back to the island republic in the 1960s, and the **Military History and Aviation Museum** has exhibits spanning the centuries and depicting military and naval activities, and more recently aviation history. The end of the peninsula is occupied by the Defence Force Headquarters and barriers manned by soldiers block the road.

Now a national park, the peninsula is managed by the Chaguaramas Development Authority. It has the responsibility for developing the area as a destination for yachtsmen and eco-tourism. The authority is also promoting the many small islands lying offshore that are separated from the mainland and each other by channels called *bocas*. Boca is the Spanish word for mouth, and the jagged islands and area around them are known as **The Dragon's Mouth**. Chaguaramas comes from the Arawak word for palm trees that used to fringe the bay, and Indians are believed to have first settled the area around 100AD. The Authority's offices are on Airways Road, Chaguaramas, and contain a small museum and interpretive facility about the area, its history and flora and fauna. Each year about 200 school groups visit the museum to learn more about the national park and the importance of eco-education.

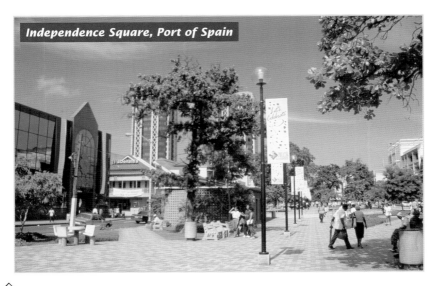

Independence Square, Port of Spain

Right top:
Queens Royal
College,
Savannah

Right below:
Stollmeyer
Castle,
Savannah

Bottom:
Gingerbread
House,
Savannah

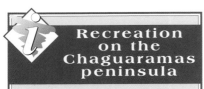

Recreation on the Chaguaramas peninsula

You can hike the 4.5 mile (7km) trail through Tucker Woods to a ridge 1600ft (530m) above sea level and then trek down to the north coast, or walk along the Covigne Rover through a nutmeg grove to water falls and a bathing pool where you can cool off, or visit the 540ft (180m) high Edith Falls at the end of a 1-mile (1.6km) trail. The Tucker Valley is also the home of the Chaguaramas Golf Course at Edith Falls. The 9-hole course was built by American servicemen during World War II and is now being expanded into an 18-hole championship course. Howler monkeys are one of the more unusual hazards while playing.

Three rivers drain the peninsula. The Cuesa is the largest. The wide valley has many huge stands of bamboo and a rich wildlife, especially close to the water with caiman, large crabs, turtles, red howler and capuchin monkeys and many species of exotic birds. There is a swamp where the river meets the sea and more excellent birding. The peninsula, locally referred as Chag, has become increasingly popular in the last few years as marina and tourism expansion has taken place.

The Kayak Centre offers kayak rentals and sightseeing tours. There are many beaches around the peninsula where you can cool off and take a swim, and among the best are **Chagville** in the south coast and **Macqueripe** on the north west coast with its secluded sandy beach.

From Port of Spain the road west is known as the **Carenage** because it was here that ships used to be beached and pulled over on their sides so their hulls could be cleaned. After the Carenage is **Welcome Bay** and **Harts Cut**, two sheltered coves that offer safe anchorages. The road then passes **Williams Bay** and secluded **Scotland Bay** that is backed by lush vegetation covered hills. **Morne Catherine** is one of the country's best bird watching spots with more than 100 species recorded and regular sightings of rare visitors. There are trails to the summit, steep and slippery in places, and access is by permit only. Check with your hotel, tourist office or tour operator about visiting and it really does pay to go with an experienced guide because you will get so much more out of your trip.

Off the western tip of the peninsula is the **Boca de Monos** which separates the mainland from the island of **Monos** which has a number of holiday cottages. Beyond that is the **Boca de Huevos**, and then in succession, the island of **Huevos, Boca De Navios** and the island of **Chacachacare**, the most westerly in the chain. You can hike to the lighthouse on the northern coast or trek south to the Salt Lake where the iguanas grow to more than 6ft (2m) in length. Although the island of Chacachacare is now protected as a nature reserve, it is possible to camp there or cross by boat to spend a day on one of the many secluded coves. It was not so popular in olden times because its isolation made it ideal as a leper colony.

Off the south coast of the peninsula are several more islands. Five Islands are closest to the Port of Spain, and to the west are the Diego Islands and beyond that **Gaspar Grande**, also known as Gasparee.

Gaspar Grande

G aspar Grande is a small island off Chaguaramas that has become a popular get away for Trinidadians, some of whom have built holiday cottages that can only be reached by boat. There used to be a whaling station on the island and you can often see dolphins in the channel, and it is now most noted for the underground sea Gasparee caves. The island makes a good picnic spot and there are the remains of old colonial military buildings and fortifications. Boats are available for the short crossing from Point Baleine, a former whaling station which prospered in the late eighteenth and nineteenth centuries, and there are tour guides for visits to the caves which are noted for their limestone formations and deep pools. The caves are open from 9am to 2.30pm during the week, and from 9am to 3pm at weekends ☎ 634-4364. The other island in the chain is Carrera, a prison colony housing prisoners on death row.

Trinidad's best beaches are on the north coast and the most popular is **Maracas Beach**, a stunning one-mile (1.6km) long golden beach often called Port of Spain's playground. It is just over half an hour's drive from the capital. The wide, white sand beach, fringed by palm trees, has the rain forest clad mountains as the spectacular backdrop. There are beach bars and the chance to try a Trinidad specialty – shark and bake, which is seasoned shark in a freshly cooked roll, with optional pepper and tamarind sauce. Take care, however, because the sauce can have more bite than the shark! Nearby **Timberline Nature Resort** offers accommodation and local sightseeing tours. The beach is a great place to see and be seen, and loitering about is a popular pastime, especially at the weekends, as the men flirt with the girls. Just to the west is **La Vache Bay**, an area noted for its scenic beauty.

There are other beaches along the north coast, and most are less busy although they are less sheltered as well. The exception is **Las Cuevas** (named after its underwater caves) that is another beach popular with Port of Spain residents at weekends and on holidays. It is only a short drive from the capital, and as with Maracas, liming is a well-liked weekend pastime. Cannons on the headland mark the site of Fort Abercromby. A good hike inland from Las Cuevas is to the **Rincon Waterfalls**. Just east of Maracas Bay is **Tyrico Bay**, a popular spot for overnight camping.

The beaches along the north coast are frequented by surfers especially when the Atlantic waves are running high. When the rollers are really good, the word goes out and impromptu camps are set up along the beach so that the surfers can surf from dawn to dusk.

From Maracas Bay it is possible

Above:
Blanchisseuse,
North coast

Right: Las Cuevas
fishing village

Below: Paria
waterfall

to hike to the 300ft (91m) **Maracas Falls** and then continue to the summit of **El Tucuche**, the country's second highest mountain in the Northern Range. The easiest hike to the Maracas Falls, however, is from the south off Eastern Main Road and into the hills via St. Joseph.

The twisting, narrow north coast road runs out at Blanchisseuse and you have either to retrace your route, or return over the northern mountain range to Arima, and then take Eastern Main Road back to Port of Spain.

Blanchisseuse

The sprawling fishing village of **Blanchisseuse** is on the north coast at the end of the road and is another good nature watching spot, especially to the east along the Marianne River from the iron bridge to its mouth. Green kingfishers can be spotted among the bamboos, and gray kingbird and yellow oriole in the coconut palms. The village hugs the coastline and the forested hills behind reach down almost to the water's edge. To the west of the village by the Damier River there is a look out over the cliffs and the sandy beaches where you can enjoy a swim.

The village name comes from the French word for a washerwoman, and wherever a river flows close to populated areas, you can often see women doing their washing with the clothes draped out to dry on rocks and bushes. Some people, however, claim that the village gets its name from the crashing white surf that can be seen along this rugged stretch of coastline. It is wonderful to sit and watch the fishermen expertly guiding their boats between the reefs and the rocks to land their catches, and then hauling the boats up the cliff side, high above the water.

From Blanchisseuse it is possible to explore further along the coast on foot or along some stretches in a four wheel drive vehicle. There is an unpaved trail that passes Morne Poui Bay, and **Paria Bay** with the **Paria Waterfall** a little way inland. This stretch of coastline beyond Blanchisseuse is not often on the tourist itinerary, but it is well worth the effort hiking as far as Paria Bay with its lovely, unspoiled beach, and the Paria Waterfall that cascades down into a rock pool. If planning to walk to the falls, take your lunch and lots of drink, and make a day of it. It takes about an hour to hike in from the road.

Another exciting way of exploring is by kayak and Kayak Tours offers wilderness tours along this stretch of coastline. It is hard work paddling your way through the surf and you must be fit, but it is a great experience and basic training is offered in one- and two-man kayaks before setting out.

The track then continues past **Madamas Bay** that makes a great campsite. The best way to get to Madamas Bay is to ask a boat from Blanchisseuse to ferry you along the coast. It is a long way to hike from Blanchisseuse but if you are used to backpacking and walking in heat, it is possible. You can also reach the bay and the river mouth from Matelot. Inland from Madamas Bay there are the **Madamas Falls**. The trail then continues east along the coast to Grande Matelot Point and the small fishing and farming village of **Matelot**, at the mouth of the Shark River, which is about a three hour drive from Port of Spain. At Matelot you re-join the paved highway which runs to Grande Riviere Point and the Mt Plaisir Estate and then on to **Sans Souci Bay** and **Salibia Bay** which offer good surfing, close to Galera Point on the north eastern corner of the island. An old light-house stands on the point overlook-ing the area where the Atlantic Ocean meets the Caribbean.

Turtle watching

The beaches along this stretch of coastline are a good place to spot giant leatherback turtles coming ashore to nest between March and September. While this wonderful spectacle should not be missed if you get the chance, you must get permission first from the Wildlife Section of the Forestry Division (☎ 662-5114) who will issue you a permit.

The Toco Main Road then runs south down the north east coast to Redhead past the **Rio Seco Water-falls** and Saline Bay to **Matura**, an-other giant leatherback turtle watch area. The gentle giants lumber ashore to bury their eggs in the sands of Matura Bay between March and August. The beach is patrolled dur-ing the egg laying period by a vol-unteer group called Nature Seekers (☎ 668-0171), and its members will act as guides if you want to go out at night to see this miracle of nature.

Remember advance permission is needed from the Wildlife Section of the Forestry Division (☎ 662-5114). The turtle watch season extends until September when the last eggs hatch and the young turtles scam-per across the sands for the safety of the ocean.

From Matura you can take the Valencia Road which runs west through Valencia and Arima back to Port of Spain. For those venturing along the north west coast as far as Blanchisseuse the choice is either to return the way you came, or to head south. From Blanchisseuse it is an exciting drive through the mountain rain forests of the **Northern Ridge** from Blanchisseuse to Arima. It offers a number of fabulous oppor-tunities to see Trinidad's diverse plant and wildlife, especially if you make stops at the **Asa Wright Na-ture Centre** and at **Andrews Trace**.

The Northern Ridge is the high-est extension of the Andes Moun-tain Range on Trinidad and the tall-est peaks are **Cerro del Aripo**, the tallest at 3083ft (940m), which is south east of Paria Bay, and **El Tucuche** that is north east of Ma-raval. More than 2,300 acres (920 hectares), around El Tucuche is now protected as a sanctuary. Of special interest are golden tree frogs, or-ange-billed nightingale thrushes and many species of exotic orchid.

You can hike to the summit of either if you are fit but take your time. Apart from the wonderful lush vegetation, you can spot a wide range of animal life from deer, wild pig, anteaters, agouti and opossum. It is also interesting to notice the vegetation changes as you climb through different altitudes from the lower montane vegetation to the rich, tropical rainforests and then finally, near the summit, to the elfin woodlands. If you plan a trip into the Northern Range, especially to either of the summits, it is a good idea to hire a guide for the trip as it is safer and you will see far more things than if you were on your own.

You can find guides in Aripo. The Aripo Caves that run for more than 300ft (91m) into the mountains are also worth a visit and day trips can be arranged.

Asa Wright's Nature Centre is on the working Spring Hill Estate at

THE TOBAGO HERITAGE FESTIVAL

The Tobago Heritage Festival which takes place over two weeks in July offers one of the best chances to see the many and different cultural facets of the island. Although the majority of the population is of African origin, the island has changed hands about thirty times until it fell under permanent English control in 1803. Apart from the English, the Spanish, French, Dutch and the Courlanders from Latvia have ruled the island.

This has led to a fascinating mix of cultures, traditions, music and rituals. In fact, many villages are unique in that they have their own music, song, dance and other traditions. That is why the festival is so interesting, because the events are planned all around the island to reflect this diversity. Festival highlights include the Bele Festival, an Old Time Tobago Wedding, Saraka Feast and the folk tale sessions. On Family Day, however, the islanders gather in Scarborough to celebrate their common heritage as Tobagonians.

Another festival highlight is the old-time Carnival, which is in total contrast to the modern Carnival of Trinidad. Carnival on Tobago stems from the French planters' commemoration of Mardi Gras, and was later adapted by the islanders to be a celebration of freedom. Several other European influences can be heard in the sea songs and dances, which include jigs and reels, a legacy of the early British settlers.

The Heritage Festival also celebrates the island's African roots, with religious ceremonies and rituals, such as the limbo dance that was traditionally performed following a funeral – symbolizing the passing of the spirit from this world to the next. Fishing villages re-enact traditional boat christenings while harvest rituals including cane grinding and cocoa harvesting, are showcased in the villages on former plantations. Storytelling is another major part of the festival, and a part of Tobago life for centuries, and it is a good way to learn of the island's myths, superstitions and folklore, and characters such as Papa Bois, Mama Dlo, (pronounced Der-low), Phantom, Doven, Soucouyant and La Diablesse.

Finally, food is another staple ingredient of the celebrations with traditional cooking methods used to prepare cassava, plantains, yams, dasheen and corn, and, of course, the ceremonial pig roast.

an altitude of 1200ft (366m), and is about 7 miles (11km) north of Arima. It is less than 90 minutes' drive from Port of Spain and the entrance is by the 7.5-mile mark on the Blanchisseuse Road. The Centre was established in 1967 with an international Board of Management, to provide a recreation and study area relating to tropical wildlife, open to all. Conservation and preservation of the habitat and species is a major role of the Centre. It covers 200 acres (80 hectares) with several nature trails through the rain forest – lasting from a few minutes to two or three hours – but you can also spot an amazing number of birds from the veranda where you can sit in the shade and enjoy a cool drink or a nice cup of tea. From your chair you can see squirrel cuckoos, toucans, tufted coquettes, trogons, motmots, antshrikes and several of the eighteen species of humming

bird found on the reserve.

The Spring Hill Estate is a working cocoa, coffee and citrus farm surrounded by tropical rain forest and towering trees with the canopy in some places as high as 150ft (46m). The area usually receives more than 90in (225cm) of rain a year which accounts for the lush, dense vegetation which in turn is home to teeming numbers of plants, birds and insects and a healthy population of mammals, amphibians and reptiles. Nature Centre guests are accommodated in comfortable, twin bedded rooms, each with bath, in the main house or surrounding cottages in the delightful grounds. Summer seminars are conducted with expert instructors in tropical field natural history, bird study and nature photography. A special feature is the annual Christmas-New Year holiday tour in conjunction with the official National Audubon Society

The Oilbird

Of special interest is the breeding colony of nocturnal oilbird, or guacharo, which are found in the depths of the Dunston Cave, carved out by an underground river over tens of thousands of years. It is the only known accessible colony of this species and is considered so important that the World Wildlife Fund made a major contribution towards the establishment of the estate so that the birds could be protected. The bird, normally found in South America, lives in caves and feeds on fruit, mainly the nuts of oil palms. The bird, which has a fan-like tail, broad wings and a hooked bill, uses echo location like a bat, to travel through the pitch-black caves. The bird emits a series of machine gun like clicks – up to 250 a second – which are audible to the human ear. The birds emerge from their roosting caves at night to feed and the young are born and reared in the dark on ledges high in the cliffs. It gets its name guachero (the wailer) because of its piercing shriek-like calls, and it gets the name oil bird, not because of its diet, but because South American Indians kill the birds and boil them to yield an odorless oil which is used for cooking and lights. Because of their rarity there are restrictions about visiting the cave colony site.

Above: Humming bird, Asa Wright Nature Centre
Below: Asa Wright Garden

Christmas Bird Count.

Andrews Trace is at an elevation of 2,000ft (610m) and there are lots of places to stop along the way to observe the bird life. You can spot swallow-tailed kite, common black hawk, humming birds, trogons and white bearded manakins, especially the males who make a great show of guarding their territories. Parrots are more likely to seen in the late afternoon.

Arima is a major crossroads town halfway between the east and west coasts and on main routes north, south, east and west. It also has a strong Amerindian tradition and an Arawak village has been recreated just to the west of the town in the Cleaver Woods Park. The town is the venue every year for the crowning of the Carib Queen during the Santa Rosa Festival. Amid much ritual, the Queen receives a crown of flowers. East of Arima is the village of Valencia and from here you can take the road leading to the **Hollis Reservoir** which is also a nature reserve rich in birdlife. You can obtain a permit to enter the reserve from the Water and Sewage Authority ☎ 662-2301.

The **Lopinot Complex** is in the Lopinot Valley, about 5 miles (8km) off the Eastern Main Road. It is the restored Great House of French Count Charles Joseph de Lopinot. He arrived on Trinidad in 1800 after fleeing from the slave uprisings in what is now Haiti, and established a large cocoa plantation. Many of the original crops grown have been replanted. His ghost is said to still haunt the house (now a museum) and grounds when storms rage at night. The area is one of the island centers of Parang, traditional Christmas music sung in Spanish. The

Lopinot Caves on the estate can also be explored.

The **Maracas Waterfall** is north of the village of **St. Joseph**, in the Northern Range, and is reached by taking the Maracas Royal Road from the Eastern Main Road and then walking in. The falls drop 300ft (91m) and are the highest in Trinidad. It is about one and a half miles (2.5km) to the falls along the trail. It is a lovely spot for a picnic, and offers camping and birding. St Joseph was the capital of the island until 1757 and it was deliberately located in the mountains well out of range of the guns of marauding ships and easy to defend. The capital moved to Port of Spain because the Governor did not like his house surrounded by the forests and all the wildlife. Nearby is the St. Augustine campus of the University of the West Indies.

Mount St. Benedict was founded in 1912 and is the largest Benedictine Monastery in the Caribbean. It is reached by taking St. John's Road off the Eastern Main Road. It has a wonderful location, 800ft (244m) above the village of St. Augustine, and set in lovely gardens with nature trails. The views south are incredible and there is a small guesthouse that has been offering simple, but comfortable accommodation since it was built in 1932, originally for people on retreat and more recently for eco-tourists and naturalists. The guesthouse even has a small laboratory and there is a teashop. (☎ 662-4084).

Return to Eastern Main Road and continue west. At the Valley Vue Hotel in **St. Ann's** there is a **Water Park** with three 400ft (122m) water slides rushing down into a splash pool. **Fort Picton** and **Fort Chacon** still dominate the eastern approaches to Port of Spain and from their vantage point above the suburb of Laventille, overlook the capital and its sea approaches. The road passes **Fort St. Andre** and it is then a short drive back into Port of Spain

THE EAST COAST

From Port of Spain take the Churchill Roosevelt Highway, which runs south and parallel to Eastern Main Road past Tunapuna and Arima to **Waller Field,** an old US army base and now an agricultural station. The surrounding pastures and wet meadows are a good place to see the savannah hawk, yellow hooded and red breasted blackbirds, southern lapwing, wattled jacana, cattle egret, pied water and white headed marsh tyrants and green rumped parrotlets.

The area south of Matura and east of Sangre Grande is known as the **Fishing Pond.** This is the traditional rice-growing area of Trinidad around the **Windbelt Lagoon** into which the Oropouche River and its tributary, the Caigual drain. There are paths through the mangrove woodlands that surround the lagoon.

Just south of Upper Manzanilla you can take the Plum Mitan Road inland which runs south-west through Plum Mitan, Poole and Biche with the Nariva Swamp between you and the sea. Manzanilla is the Spanish word for the manchineel, a poisonous plant commonly found on beaches. If you continue towards the coast you reach Lower Manzanilla and the fabulous **Manzanilla Bay** that stretches for almost as far as the eye can see. There are changing rooms,

Rich bird life

The village of **Cumuto** to the west of Sangre Grande is a good springboard for exploring the central savannah. The savannah south of the Eastern Main Road is particularly rich in bird life with up to seventy species recorded, including gray-headed kite, savannah hawk, parrots, red-bellied macaw, squirrel and striped cuckoos, humming birds, flycatchers, vireos, orioles, tanagers, honeycreepers, doves and many types of finch. At the northern end of the village near the Moriche Palms you can usually see fork tailed palm swifts, while in the village itself you can spot clusters of nests of the yellow-rumped cacique. In the Arena Forest there are species of trogons, woodpeckers, woodcreepers and tanagers, and it is the best place to see rufus tailed jacamars.

showers and a snack bar.

The beautiful Manzanilla-Mayaro Road runs for 5 miles (8km) beside the sea and through a huge coconut grove that runs alongside **Cocos Bay,** which is really one long glorious palm-fringed sand beach. The coconut groves were once an important part of the island's economy, but most of the palms are now self-sown, springing up where the coconuts fall to the ground. Areas between the palms have been cleared, however, for growing vegetables and watermelons. **Mayaro Bay** is the longest stretch of beach

Four-eyed fish

If you stop and study the surf at Mayaro Bay you can sometimes see four eyed fish (Anableps) in the water. This amazing species lives on the surface of the water and has specially adapted eyes, the top half of which allows it to see above the water level, while with the bottom half it can see below the surface. The fish grows up to 12in (30cm) in length.

in Trinidad and has a number of guesthouses and hotels.

As you travel further down the coast road you have the sea on your left and the vast swamplands on the right of the road. The **Nariva Swamp** on the east coast is reached by traveling south from Lower Manzanillo or north from Mayaro. This area of swamp wetlands is an internationally known wildlife site and protected habitat with the island's only remaining population of macaws in the wild. They can usually be seen late in the day returning to their roosts high up in the cabbage palms. It includes the **Bush Sanctuary** and **Cocal Kernahan** wetlands. Its rich wildlife includes red howler and white capuchin monkeys, the latter unique to Trinidad, and hundreds of other species of animals, birds, reptiles and amphibians, including the endangered West Indian manatee. The area is noted for its succulent crabs and oysters. The waters also yield the cascadura, the fish which, according to legend, once tasted has the power to pull you back to the island. For tours contact the Forestry Department ☎ 662-5114.

Ortoire river, Atlantic side

Above: Blanchisseuse, North coast
Below: Mangroves, Cocos Bay

The 'Melon Patch' is a mixture of uncultivated marsh and rice paddies, and also rich in bird life with pinnated bittern, limpkin, azure gallinule, red bellied macaw, black bellied tree duck, striated heron and yellow hooded blackbird. Take a walk along the bank of Bush-bush Creek where you can see wattled jacana, fork tailed palm swift, orange winged parrot and, occasionally pearl kite and red-bellied macaw, as well as green kingfisher and green rumper parrotlet.

The Mayaro region occupies the south-east corner of the island and is drained by the Ortoire and Lizard Rivers that run to the Atlantic. **Mayaro**, formerly a small fishing village, is now a busy little oil town, thanks to the discovery of offshore oil. Amoco is the main oil company and its offshore rigs can be pinpointed at night by the flames as the vented gases are burned. The town itself has retained much of its old world charm and still has its fishing port, and it is also developing as a tourist resort for those who just want to enjoy the peace and quiet of this part of the island.

The journey back takes you through Rushville, Rio Claro and the Tabaquite Tunnel to Flanagan Town, Caparo and Mamoral. **Mundo Nuevo** is just north of Mamoral and marks the northern point of a vast nature reserve in one of the remotest parts of Trinidad.

The route continues north through the village of Talparo to **San Raphael**, a home of parang music, and the area still has some great houses from the old cocoa estates. You then connect with the Churchill Roosevelt Highway and head back to Port of Spain.

THE WEST COAST

Take the Churchill Roosevelt Highway out of Port of Spain and exit for Valsayn, and then head south for the turn off which follows the Blue River to the coast and the entrance to the Caroni Swamp.

The **Caroni Swamp** has to be explored by boat, which can negotiate between the mangrove islands in the area which is part swamp and part lagoon. It is a stunning bird watching area where European bird spotters can usually see at least twenty new species, such as neotropical cormorant, gallinules, large billed tern, anhinga, tricolored heron, striated heron, cattle egret, clapper rail, pied water tyrant, white cheeked pintail, red capped cardinal, greater ani, common potoo and bicolored conebill. One of the most memorable sights is the evening flight of egrets and scarlet ibis as the birds fly home to roost on the mangrove islands. The spectacle continues from late afternoon until sunset. You will also see hundreds of crabs that live among the mangrove roots and you might spot a boa or two. There are boat tours from late afternoon from the mouth of the Blue River.

Return to the Uriah Butler Highway and continue south to the fast-growing **Chaguanas**, the main town of the heavily industrialized and agricultural central region and its administrative center. One if the main sights is the Lion House, which was immortalized by V S Naipaul in his novel, *A House for Mr. Biswas*.

Just south of the town is the village of **Edinburgh**, which is noted for its potteries. A wide range of pots, urns and water jugs are made using traditional firing techniques that have not changed for more than

100 years. The potteries also produce the shallow *deyas*, the oil lamps used to celebrate the Hindu festival of Divali.

Inland is the **Central Range** and the **Mt Tamana** area which is a good place to see shiny and giant cowbirds, yellow oriole, yellow rumped cacique, plumbeous and gray headed kites, blue black grassquit and ruddy breasted seedeater.

Just south of Flanagan Town you make a right turn for Gran Couva and the **La Vega Estate**. La Vega Garden Centre is a lovely place to learn about the wide range of tropical fruit, flowers, plants and trees grown there, or just to enjoy a picnic. The Centre was founded in 1988 and tours can be arranged. There is a lake that offers fishing and canoeing. Then continue southwest to Gasparillo and St Madeline and on to **Princes Town.**

From Princes Town it is a short drive to the **Devil's Woodyard**, a mud volcano that can be quite vigorous at times. It is difficult to find but if you ask for directions in Princes Town they will be gladly given. Continued on page 65.

The Company Villages

Princes Town is on the road from San Fernando that runs across country through Rico Claro to Mayaro, and just to the east there is a road that runs south through **Third Company**, one of a cluster of settlements known as the Company Villages. The origin of their names is disputed. One story is that plantation owners built them in the nineteenth century to house their 'regiments' of slaves. Another version is that they were named after Afro-American Regiments brought to Trinidad from the US in the middle of the nineteenth century. This version adds that there is no Second Company village because their ship foundered and all the men were lost at sea.

Sugar cane country

Sugar cane country is in the heart of central Trinidad which extends north to the iron bridge over the Caroni River near Valsayn, south and west, and which has traditionally been the island's breadbasket, growing sugar cane and cocoa, for many years the mainstay of the economy. As you head inland towards Caparo, it is still common to see ox carts on the country roads, especially during the harvest when they are laden with sugar cane. Chaguanas is still growing fast but as you travel inland there are mostly small farming villages, most of them with predominantly East Indian populations who speak Hindi as their first language. As you travel south from Valsayn there is mile after mile of sugar cane fields on your left, and if you detour into this area, you can visit the sugar cane villages of Caroni on the river of the same name, Cunupia, Caparo and many others. A couple of miles east of the town is the village of Longdenville and the Brasso to Tabaquite Road which runs south east. This road is one of the most scenic in Trinidad and runs through the Caparo Valley with its citrus groves, and then up into the wooded Montserrat Hills. Further inland there are many old cocoa estates and you can see the cocoa sheds with their sliding sheds that allowed the beans to be dried in the sun.

Carnival was born in Trinidad and the island is still the home of the biggest, best, loudest and most vibrant carnival in the Caribbean. Although the festivities last for just two frenetic days of costume parades, music and partying before Lent, the preparations take months, and reach a crescendo in the weeks after Christmas. Carnival season starts on New Year's Day and during this pre-festival period, costumes are completed, songs rehearsed, new calypsos aired, and elaborate dance routines practised. Carnival itself is an occasion not to be missed with the activities starting on Friday and running over the weekend, with the main events on Carnival Monday and Carnival Tuesday – the day before Ash Wednesday and the official start of Lent – when you *play mas*, take part in the great masquerade. Mas is an abbreviation of masquerade, which was a grand ball held by the European gentry. The participants wore their finest costumes and gems but hid their identities behind masques (face masks). French settlers introduced the custom to Trinidad in the late 1700s. They would parade from house to house wearing their masks.

On Carnival Monday, revellers take to the streets as early as 2am wearing *ole mas* (old costumes), while some wear rags and daub themselves with mud. This is part of the J'ouvert celebration (a contraction of the French words *jour* and *ouvert* literally meaning day opening or dawn), and is in sharp contrast to the splendid costumes that come later, but is a spectacle in its own right with dancing, and loud, loud music. The Savannah is at the heart of the celebrations and on Shrove Tuesday, loud-speaker-carrying trucks and costumed marchers make their way through the streets led by a wicked looking devil, followed by the highlight of Carnival, the parade of the bands with thousands upon thousands of musicians and supporters. The bands make their way to the Savannah where the judging takes place.

Carnival stems from the much more sober pre-Lenten Roman Catholic ceremonies practised by the French aristocracy two centuries ago. After Emancipation, however, the ceremony became an exuberant celebration of freedom, and it still is. The costumes, both adults and children's, are stunning and only matched by the body painting and the exuberance of the participants. Carnival on Trinidad is focussed on the Savannah where truck borne musicians compete with the blasting speakers of the DJs, and the costumed bands. There are Calypso contests to find the Calypso Monarch, and the pulsating, almost hypnotic rhythms of soca, as well as the steel bands whose members,

sometimes 100 and more, playing perhaps 200 or more pans, produce the most extraordinary and beautiful sounds, and compete for the prestigious title of Panorama Champion.

Earlier in February, there is the Pan Around the Neck festival, which is really a prelude to Carnival. Originally steel bands were not stationary and the pan (steel drum) was carried by a strap that went around the neck. The steel pan originated in the back streets of Port of Spain about fifty years ago, and is believed to be the only new musical instrument created this century. The plantation owners outlawed African drums because they thought the slaves used them for sending messages to each other, and so alternative drums were created using gourds, goatskins and whatever else was suitable. The steel pan is the latest manifestation of this ingenuity, and is now an integral part of Trinidad and Tobago's music and culture. While traditional steel band music is truly Caribbean in essence, the musicians are often very talented, and can play wonderful classical music and jazz, an illustration of how versatile the steel pan is.

Continued over page...

And, in May, there is Pan Ramajay, a festival for the smaller steel bands to showcase their talents. Every September, Trinidad also hosts the Carnival King and Queen of the World Competition.

There are more than 100 pan yards throughout Trinidad and Tobago where you can watch and hear the musicians practise. They have great names such as Scrunters Pan Groove, Valley Harps and the WITCO Desperadoes in Port of Spain. There are monthly pan concerts at the Amoco Renegades Pan Theatre, in Charlotte Street, Port of Spain.

For more information about Carnival, you can contact the National Carnival Commission, 82-84 Frederick Street, Port of Spain ☎ 623-8867, and about the pan bands, contact Pan Trinbago, 75 Edward Street, Port of Spain ☎ 623-4486.

Calypso

Trinidad is the home of calypso, or kaiso, which celebrates news events, politics and gossip, and while it may be difficult to catch all the lyrics, you will love the beat.

The calypso is a folk song and the lyrics can range from witty and satirical to mocking and full of double entendres – and no one, no matter how famous or important, is immune. The calypso tradition, which has now spread throughout the southern and eastern Caribbean, became popular internationally in the 1950s, but dates from the early nineteenth century in the Caribbean and has its roots in West African music. During the carnival season before Lent, slave choirs called shatwell, would wander through the streets singing improvised songs, mostly about unpopular political figures.

Calypsos are sung year round, but really come into their own at Carnival Time when the island's best vie for the title of Calypso King. You can pop in to one of the many calypso 'tents' (now halls) where hundreds of calypsos are sung, and only the most popular make it to the finals when the most popular singer is voted king.

The basic form of calypso is similar to the ballad with a four-line refrain followed by an eight-line stanza set to either a standard or original melody. Lyrics incorporate highly original and exaggerated language and patois, and the singers adopt equally original stage names such as the Mighty Spoiler, Lord Melody, Black Stalin, and perhaps the most famous of them all, the Mighty Sparrow. Popular accompanying instruments include the shak-shak or maraca guitar, the four stringed Spanish cuatro, and tamboo-tamboo, bamboo poles of varying lengths stuck in the ground, and since the 1950s, steel bands. The beat that pulsates at Carnival time is usually soca, a blend of traditional Calypso and American soul, while chutney, which is a blend with Indian music, is also becoming increasingly popular. Good places to listen to calypso are Wazo Deyzeel, Moon over Bourbon Street, Mas Camp Pub and Soca Boat at the cruise ship terminal.

The road continues south through Basse Terre to the coast and Moruga. **Moruga** is another quiet fishing village with an old church a short distance inland from the sea. Every year there is a re-enactment of Columbus's landing on the island. From Moruga you have to return inland though Basse Terre and then turn left on to Rock Road for Sadhoowa.

Penal is a traditional Trinidadian village and has changed little over the decades. Penal and similar rustic villages such as Monkey Town are worth visiting because they show what life has been like on the island for several generations. They are also great places to get to know the locals over a drink of rum in the rumshop, or while tasting some spicy roti. The Penal Road that runs north to Canaan just south of San Fernando, also passes through the small village of **Debe** which has a reputation for its traditional Indian fare.

Island saint

Siparia is most famous as the home of the Black Virgin, a revered island saint. The statue of La Divina Pastora is said to have the power to effect miracles and it is worshipped by both Christians and Hindus. The Festival of La Divina Pastora takes place shortly after Easter.

From Siparia the Siparia Road runs north to Fyzabad that is the heart of Trinidad's oil belt. Oil and natural gas have been discovered deep underground throughout this re-gion as far south as Erin Point on the coast, and you can still see the derricks pumping out their liquid gold. From Siparia you can drive south to **Quinam Beach** and the new **Quinam Recreation Park,** an eco-park in a forested area with information building and nature trails.

Continue through Palo Seco and San Francique to Buenos Ayres then northwest along Erin Road to its junction with the Southern Trunk Road. Turn left and head through this remote, undisturbed area for the end of the peninsula. Just past Bonasse the road starts to deteriorate but you can continue past more mud volcanoes and through old coconut estates to **Icacos**, a small fishing village that is at the southwest tip of Trinidad. From the coast it is usually possible to see the Venezuelan coast very clearly just 7 miles (11km) away. You can usually buy fish straight from the fishing boats as they land their catches. It is just south of Columbus Bay where the explorer is said to have landed on 31 July 1498 during his third voyage of discovery. There is a trail from the road to the bay.

The route then heads back north to Point Fortin, now very much a coastal oil town but with little to see. The road from the Cedros region to La Brea is quite twisting and bumpy and some care needs to be taken. It is not a road to be rushed.

One of the island's main natural attractions is just outside the town of **La Brea. The Pitch Lake** is a 100-acre (40-hecatre) lake you can actually walk on – with care – because it is consists of thick pitch and, it is able to replenish itself. The pitch is really crude oil and bitumen constantly seeps up through a fault in the sandstone 250ft (76m) below the ground. Every time pitch is removed for export and to repair roads and make asphalt roofs, the lake, the largest of its kind in the world, tops itself up, and it has been doing so ever since explorer and privateer Sir Walter Raleigh used the pitch to repair his fleet in the late 1500s. He even took some back to repair the road across Westminster Bridge but it did not set. Today the pitch is scooped out, loaded on to railway carriages and exported around the world. There are guides to show you around for a charge, and there is a small museum.

The coastal road is quite twisty and it takes about 40 minutes to travel from La Brea to **San Fernando**, past the **Oropuche Lagoon**.

History of San Fernando

San Fernando is Trinidad's second largest city and was founded and named in 1786 in honor of Ferdinand of Asturias, the infant son of the king who later became Ferdinand VII. It was settled following a land grant and was the site of a Capuchin Mission. The town was destroyed by a fire in 1818 but rebuilt within its present boundaries.

The city is the administrative and trading hub for the south of the island, and the focus of the island's oil and gas industries with its own port, and with vast plants at Point Lisas and Pointe-a-Pierre, to the north, where the product is ex-

ported by ship. It is at the western end of the Central Range on the Gulf of Paria

The city is less than an hour's drive from Port of Spain through sugar cane fields and several small villages where you can see traditional craftsmen at work. The fastest way to reach the city is by the Uriah Butler Highway and if you do not have your own car, you can take a taxi or catch the express bus that runs between Port of Spain and San Fernando.

The city is built on the hillside overlooking the sea. The High Street runs from the wharf and climbs up to Library Corner where you can find taxis and all sorts of street venders and fast food outlets. High Street itself largely consists of bazaar-type shops and Trinidadian fast food stalls, and running parallel with it is Harris Promenade, named after former British Colonial Governor Lord Harris. Along the Promenade and in a line are the Roman Catholic, Methodist and Anglican Churches, as well as the Town Hall and City Council. There is also a statue of Mahatma Ghandi, and, rather strangely an old railway engine. Local wits will tell you that the steam engine is 'the last train to San Fernando' but it was one of the many trains used to haul sugar cane on plantations throughout the island.

Although San Fernando is the country's second city, it has not developed in the same orderly way as Port of Spain. It is quite easy to lose your way in the warren of streets away from High Street and Harris Promenade, although you can't get truly lost because you know the city is on a hill and if you descend you will eventually reach the waterfront.

Lush tropical vegetation typical along the west coast

The fish market is worth a visit, especially in the afternoon when the day's catch is being sold and, you can later enjoy the fish at one of the city's many restaurants. There are a number of Chinese restaurants, including Soong's Great Wall, and several other cuisines to choose from such as Middle Eastern and East Indian roti shops, reflecting its high East Indian population. The Tree House offers more elegant dining with an international menu. There are also many bars offering music and dancing, and among the most popular is The Club in the Gulf City Shopping Complex. On the outskirts of town is **Palmiste National Park** with jogging trails, picnic areas, eco-trails and an arboretum.

It is worth driving up **San Fernando Hill** that overlooks the city and the sea, and much of the Naparima Plain to the south. The hill, which is looked after by the Forestry Division, has little vegetation as much of it has been removed during the course of extensive quarrying, but apart from the views there are hiking trails and a new visitor facility. There are usually rangers on duty at the Great Wall entrance. It is known that there was a Carib settlement on the coast in the area now occupied by the city, and San Fernando hill is believed to have been an important Amerindian ritual site.

The **Point-a-Pierre Wildfowl Trust** is a research and conservation facility on 65 acres (26 hectares) of land that is part of the Petrotrin Oil Refinery on the west coast. It has lakes, nature trails and a learning facility, and the trust is dedicated to protecting endangered waterfowl and birds and through a breeding schedule, re-introducing them into the wild. The lakes support a rich array of wildfowl including the red billed whistling tree duck and the Bahama pintail, and have their own exotic vegetation with lotus flowers and water lilies.

Continue to Couva and it is worth detouring to **Waterloo**, a pretty village on the coast approached by an impressive road lined with towering royal palms. Some way offshore is **Shiv Mandir**, a floating Hindu temple, a memorial to one man's devoutness. The temple was built single-handedly by workman Siewdath Sadhu in the 1930s. He built it at sea because he did not own any land and could not get permission to construct it ashore. His statue stands in the carp ark looking out to his work in the sea.

Return to Chaguanas and take the Uriah Butler Highway north to Valsayn and back to Port of Spain.

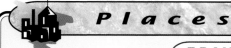
PORT OF SPAIN

Botanic Gardens

North side of the Savannah
☎ 622-1221
The Gardens are open daily from 6am to 6pm. Admission is free.

Emperor Valley Zoo

Near the Botanic Gardens
☎ 622-3530
The zoo features animals and birds found on Trinidad and Tobago, and is open daily from 9.30am to 6pm.

National Museum and Art Gallery

South-east corner of the Savannah
☎ 623-5941
It is open from Tuesday to Saturday between 10am and 6pm and admission is free.

Angostura Distillery

☎ 623-1841
Tours are available on Tuesday and Thursday. Ring in advance to arrange.

NORTH COAST

Fort George

It is open daily until 6pm. Admission is free.

Military History and Aviation Museum

Chaguaramas peninsula
☎ 634-4391 It is open daily from 9am to 6pm

Asa Wright's Nature Centre

☎ 667-4655
The Centre is open daily from 9am to 5pm with guided tours at 10am and 1.30pm. Reservations for the tours are required.

Lopinot Complex

In the Lopinot Valley, about 5 miles (8km) off the Eastern Main Road
The house is now a museum and the complex is open daily from 6am to 6pm with free admission.

Water Park, Valley Vue Hotel

St Ann's
☎ 623-3511
It is open daily from 10am to 6pm.

EAST COAST

La Vega Garden Centre

south of Flanagan Town
☎ 653-6120.

Quinam Recreation Park

Quinam Bay, south of Siparia
☎ 622-3217.

THE PITCH LAKE

La Brea, North-west of Siparia

☎ 648-7697.
There are guides to show you around for a charge, and there is a small museum that is open daily from 10am to 6pm

Point-a-Pierre Wildfowl Trust

Part of the Petrotrin Oil Refinery on the west coast.
☎ 662-4040
It is open weekdays from 10am to 5pm, Saturday from noon to 4pm and Sunday from 10.30am to 6pm. There are daily tours for schoolchildren and the general public but places must be booked in advance.

$ inexpensive
$$ moderate
$$$ expensive

Port of Spain and area

Ali Baba $$
Royal Palm Plaza, Maraval.
☎ 622-5557
Arabic

Apsara $$
Grand Bazaar,
☎ 627-7364
Indian

Botticelli's $$-$$$
Grand Bazaar,
☎ 663-8733
Italian

La Boucan $$$
Trinidad Hilton,
☎ 624-3211
Fine dining with international and West Indian dishes, with buffet lunch from noon to 2.30pm, and live entertainment during afternoon tea Wednesday to Friday, and dinner nightly.

Café Trinidad $-$$
Hotel Normandie,
☎ 624-1181
Snacks, pies and pastries.

Chaconia Inn $$
106 Saddle Road, Maraval,
☎ 628-8603
Local and international dishes

China Kitchen $$
48A Ariapita Avenue, Woodbrook,
☎ 622-3756
Chinese

Chutney Rose $$
Ariapita Avenue and Fitt Street,
☎ 628-8541
Indian

Darkie's $
Queen's Park Savannah # 16,
☎ 671-7907
Local dishes

Festak $-$$
Frederick Street
Ghanaian dishes

Flag's Restaurant and Sports Lounge $$
14 Long Circular Road, Maraval,
☎ 628-3000
International cuisine in a casual dining atmosphere with sports lounge.

Flavours on the Avenue $$-$$$
Ariapita Avenue and Comelio Street,
☎ 628-8687
Nouvelle cuisine

The Gourmet Club $$$
Ellerslie Plaza,
☎ 628-5115
Fine Italian dining. Open weekdays for lunch and dinner on Saturday.

Il Colosseo $$-$$$
47 Ariapita Avenue,
☎ 623-3654
Fine Italian dining.

Indego $$
Carib Way, St. Anns,
☎ 624-6954
Caribbean and island dishes.

La Vidalia $$-$$$
The Normandie. St. Ann's,
☎ 624-1181
International and Creole.

Little Lisbon $$
7 Long Circular Road, St. James,
☎ 622-6113
Portuguese

Mr B's $$
Saddle Road, Maraval,
☎ 628-2732
Creole and seafood.

Above: Snack bar, Port of Spain
Below: Fruit punch

The Pelican Inn Restaurant $$
2-4 Coblentz Avenue, Cascade,
☎ 624-7486
An English-style pub with good value pub food and drink available from 11.30am daily. Music some nights and liming on Friday and Sunday.

Pink Anthurium $$
Saddle Road, Maraval,
☎ 628-3334
Local and Caribbean cuisine.

Rafters Restaurant $$
Woodford and Warner Streets, Port of Spain,
☎ 628-9258
Casual elegance for lunches with daily buffets, late afternoon cocktails and early evening snacks with specialty sandwiches, gourmet burgers, pasta and local seafood.

La Ronde $$-$$$
Holiday Inn, Wrightson Road,
☎ 625-3361
Enjoy the island's only revolving restaurant serving international food and great views. Open from Tuesday to Saturday from 7pm to 11pm.

Solimar $$
6 Nook Avenue, St. Ann's,
☎ 624-6267
Open for dinners Monday to Saturday and offering innovative international fare created by owner chef Joe Brown, with good service and a good selection of wines.

Tamnak $$
Queen's Park East,
☎ 625-0647
Thai

TGI Fridays $$
Amoco Plaza,
☎ 628-8443
American

Tiki Village $$-$$$
Kapok Hotel,
☎ 622-5765
Asian and Polynesian dishes and great views from the eighth-floor restaurant.

Trees $$
58 Frederick Street,
☎ 624-8733
Italian cuisine, open weekdays for lunch.

Valpark $$
Valpark Plaza, Valsayn, Port of Spain,
☎ 662-4540
Chinese restaurant.

Veni Mange $$
Woodbrook,
☎ 624-4597
Nouvelle Trinidadian.

Verandah $$
St. Rust,
☎ 622-6287
Island cooking in a traditional-home setting.

Woodford Café $$
62 Tragarete Road, Newtown, Port of Spain,
☎ 628-2233
Serves traditional local and Caribbean cuisine, closed Sunday.

Blanchisseuse

Cocos Hut $$
Laguna Mar Resort, Paria Main Road,
☎ 628-3737
Local dishes and seafood.

Chaguaramas

The Anchorage $$
Point Gourde Road, Small Boats,
☎ 634-4334
Good value menu featuring local seafood and international dishes.

The Bight $$
Western Main Road,
☎ 634-4423
Seafood, steaks and snacks.

Lighthouse $$
CrewsInn Marina,
☎ 634-4384
Open air dining offering a blend of
French, American and West Indian
cuisine.

San Fernando

Canton Palace $$
Cross Crossing Shopping Centre,
☎ 652-5993
Chinese restaurant open Monday to
Saturday 11am to 10pm, and Sunday
from 11am to 2pm for take away
only.

Family Tree House $$
London Street, St. Joseph Village,
☎ 653-8733
Cajun and international dining.

Jenny's Wok and Steakhouse $$
Cipero Road,
☎ 652-1807
Chinese-American.

Shish Kebab $-$$
Cross Shopping Centre, Upper Level,
☎ 652-4069
Steaks, seafood and kebabs.

Soong's Great Wall $$
97 Circular Road,
☎ 657-5050
Chinese cooking available daily with
good value, Wednesday night buffet
and nightly entertainment.

NIGHTLIFE

Most of the real action is in and
around Port of Spain although
Maraval and Chaguaramas have some
lively bars and hangouts. Check out,
The Anchorage, Pier I and The Base,
on Carenage; Bois Cano, Kapok
Hotel; Club Coconuts, St. Anns; Club
Liquid, Maritime Centre, Barataria;
Island Club Casino, Grand Bazaar;
Jazzy's, Western Main Road; Martin's
on the Boulevard, Cipriani Boule-
vard; Moon Over Bourbon Street,
West Mall; Mas Camp Pub,
Wrightson Road, Pelican Inn,
Cascade; Ragoo's, Ariapita Avenue
and Smokey & Bunty's, Western
Main Road.

The best way to sum up this delightful island is that it is truly laid back, very relaxing, friendly, with great charm and lovely unspoiled beaches. Pigeon Point and Store Bay are the most popular beaches and, generally, the western Caribbean beaches are calmer than those on the eastern Atlantic coast.

The island has come a long way fast considering that it did not have a regular sea link with Trinidad until 1920, and that electricity did not arrive until the 1950s. Today, Tobago offers luxury resorts and world-class scuba diving although this fact has yet to be discovered by most divers. It offers superb bird watching and great food. You can take day cruises, watch the reefs on a glass bottom boat, sail, water-ski or windsurf. Most dive shops offer beginner scuba courses that can be completed within a day, with more advanced certification available.

There is internationally-acclaimed deep sea fishing for sailfish, tarpon, tuna and wahoo, and the annual Carib International Game Fishing Tournament, held in late April or early May, attracts top international anglers. If you are a landlubber, there is golf at the Mount Irvine 18-hole championship course, rated one of the best in the world, plus tennis, hiking and horseback riding from the Palm Tree Village Vacation Club. There is also world class birding with 400 species of Caribbean, Central and South American birds listed. The island has some very large lizards and iguana, and twenty-four species of snake – but none of them is poisonous – and four species of sea turtle nest on the island's beaches between March and July.

Most of the resort hotels have their own shops and boutiques, and while Scarborough has a number of interesting stores best buys are arts, crafts and island designed batiks – you can see them being produced at the Cotton House in Scarborough. The following galleries are also worth a visit: Kimme's Sculpture Museum, Mt. Irvine ☎ 673-0604; Art Gallery and Tea Garden, Store Bay ☎ 639-8535; and Tobago Museum, King Street, Scarborough ☎ 639-3970.

The word Tobago is said to derive from the Carib word for tobacco although it is more likely to have come from their word for the pipe they used. The island motto *pulchrior evenit* (she becomes more beautiful) needs no explanation. For 300 years, the island was divided into wealthy plantations and many of the great houses remain, together with waterwheels, old sugar mills and other estate equipment. There are also great hiking and nature trails both along the coast and in the hilly, tropical rain forests. Although these trails are clear to follow, it is a good idea to be accompanied by an experienced island guide because you will get so much more from your day out – and will get back on time.

SCARBOROUGH

Tobago has a population of about 45,000 and **Scarborough**, with a population of around 25,000, is the main settlement and the island's market town on the south-east coast. It has been the capital since 1769 when the British moved it from Georgetown, which was founded in 1763 just inland from Granby Point. The authorities had wanted to develop Plymouth as the island's new capital and main port, but John Simpson, owner of the Courland Estate and Speaker of the House of Assembly, is said to have forced the move to Georgetown as Plymouth was too close to his estate, and he feared his slaves would be corrupted by the grog shops and sailors frequenting them. Georgetown turned out to be a poor choice so the capital was moved again to Scarborough.

The town nestles in **Rockly Bay** that was originally called Roode Klyp Bay by the Dutch, then Red Cliff Bay by the British before changing to Rockly. The streets lead up the hillside from the port that houses the Scarborough Cruise Ship Complex and the ferry terminal. When a ferry or cruise ship is in town the area is packed with stalls, taxis and people. The oldest part of town is by the waterside and is known as Lower Scarborough or Downtown, and there have been European settlements here for at least 300 years, with possible early Amerindian villages.

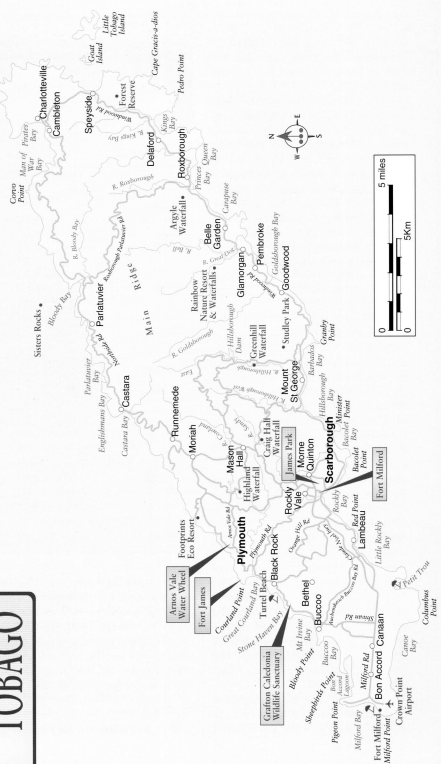

TOBAGO

Giles Island

Sisters Rocks

Corvo Point

Man of War Bay

Pirates Bay

Charlotteville

Cambleton

Speyside

Goat Island

Little Tobago Island

Cape Gracis-a-dios

Pedro Point

Forest Reserve

Windwood Rd

Kings Bay

R. Kings Bay

Delaford

Roxborough

R. Roxborough

Princes Bay

Queen Bay

Carapuse Bay

Bloody Bay

R. Bloody Bay

Parlatuvier

Parlatuvier Bay

Northside Rd

Argyle Waterfall

Belle Garden

Goldsborough Bay

Pembroke

Goodwood

Windwood Rd

Main Ridge

Roxborough Parlatuvier Rd

R. Bell

R. Great Dog

Rainbow Nature Resort & Waterfalls

Glamorgan

Studley Park

Granby Point

Englishmans Bay

Castara Bay

Castara

Runnemede

R. Goldsborough

East

Hillsborough Dam

Greenhill Waterfall

R. Hillsborough West

Barbados Bay

Moriah

Mason Hall

R. Courland

R. Sandy

Mount St George

Hillsborough Bay

Minister Point

Bacolet Point

Footprints Eco Resort

Arnos Vale Rd

Plymouth

Craig Hall Waterfall

James Park

Morne Quinton

Scarborough

Bacolet Point

Arnos Vale Water Wheel

Highland Waterfall

Rockly Vale

Rockly Bay

Fort Milford

Fort James

Plymouth Rd

Black Rock

Orange Hill Rd

Red Point

Lambeau

Little Rockly Bay

Courland Point

Turtel Beach

Great Courland Bay

Bethel

Buccoo

Auchenskeoch Buccoo Bay Rd

Claude Noel Hwy

Petit Trou

Columbus Point

Stone Haven Bay

Grafton Caledonia Wildlife Sanctuary

Bloody Point

Mt Irvine Bay

Buccoo Bay

Shirvan Rd

Canaan

Canoe Bay

Sheephirds Point

Buccoo Accord Lagoon

Milford Rd

Bon Accord

Crown Point Airport

Pigeon Point

Fort Milford

Milford Point

Milford Rd

N
E
S
W

5 miles

5Km

0

The best way to see the island is by hire car or taxi. Sightseeing tours by taxi offer a good way to get to the more out of the way places, and rates are generally negotiable. It becomes very affordable if a number of you are sharing the cost. If hiring a car, remember that garages are few and far between in rural areas and those that there are close early and do not open on Sunday.

There are public-run PTSC buses on all the major routes from Scarborough to Plymouth, Crown Point and the west end of the island but none to the east end. The buses are cheap and run reasonably frequently, but you do not have the flexibility to stop and explore or take a cooling dip in the sea whenever the fancy takes you as you would if you had your own vehicle. There are also maxi-taxis and these offer the cheapest way to get to the east end, Speyside and Charlotteville.

Above: Fort King George, Scarborough

Left: Yellow Poui tree, Fort King George, Scarborough

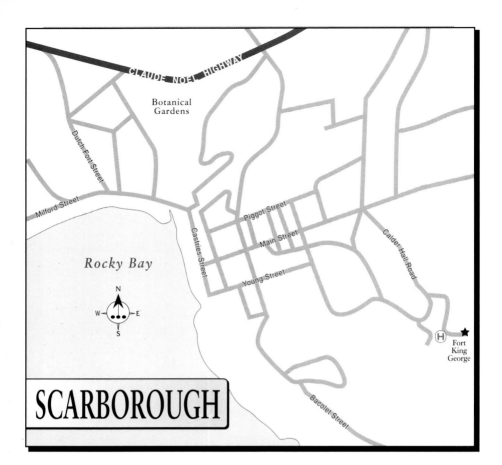

lar views and the museum. There are normally guides on hand to show you around.

The Officers Mess now houses an art studio and craft shop, and the old military hospital is now the home of the **National Fine Arts Centre**, with a wide range of island art craft. Exhibits include a bust of A. P. T. James by German sculptress Luise Kimme, who, when she is on the island, lives and works at the Fairyhaus which can be visited. The Museum of Tobago History is housed in the former Barrack Guard House and displays island history from pre-Columbian times with Amerindian exhibits dating back to 2500BC. There are also sections on the end of slavery plus military

memorabilia with maps and old photographs. The lighthouse was installed in 1958 after being transferred from Toco, Trinidad.

Scarborough Hospital nestles below the fort and has been tending the sick since 1819. Another point of interest is Scarborough Methodist Church on Fort Street that dates from 1824. The town boasts several good value, lively, informal eateries where you can enjoy island food in friendly company.

ISLAND TOUR

From Scarborough the Claude Noel Highway is the main road to the Crown Point International Airport and the more populated south-west corner of the island. The Windward Road is the main road east from Scarborough that runs to Roxborough and on to Charlotteville, while the Northside Road crosses the island through Calder Hill and past the President's Official Tobago Residence to the north coast.

Place names

One of the many interesting aspects of touring the island is the diversity of place names that are constant reminders of Tobago's exceptional history. There are English, Welsh, Scottish, French and even Carib names and most are named after their respective settlers hometowns. An exception is the village called The Whim, which lies midway between Scarborough and Plymouth. The origin of its name is unclear.

Many of the villages, especially those on the south coast east of Goodwood, tend to sprawl and often run into each other so you are never sure where one ends and the next starts. If in doubt, stop and ask. Outside Scarborough, most of the population lives in the Lowlands, which occupies the southwest quarter of the island, an area that used to be dominated by massive sugar cane plantations.

THE SOUTH-WEST CORNER

The **Claude Noel Highway**, named after the Tobagonian world light heavyweight boxing champion, runs through Palm Tree Village and Lambeau and then cuts inland through Shirvan Park and Canaan to the **Crown Point International Airport**. Just inland from **Crown Point** are the **Crusoe Caves**, claimed to be the inspiration for the Robinson Crusoe novel although there is no hard evidence for this, other than a reference in Defoe's novel: 'the Great Island on the horizon is Trinidad'.

North of Crown Point, the most south-westerly point of the island, is **Fort Milford**, built in the 1770's. It lies north of the airport and has some cannon still pointing out to sea. The road then runs past Sandy Bay and the Sandy Bay Beach Club, to **Store Bay**, a popular white sand beach area that extends to Pigeon Point. Apart from the attractions of the beach, warm sea and nearby Buccoo Reef, there are plenty of chances to try local fast food from one of the seafront stalls. Try the delicious crab and dumplings. For excellent sit down seafood, try In Seine and Dillon's. There are also changing rooms and an area where local craftsmen sell their wares. The Great Race, a power boat race, takes place off Store Bay every year.

Pigeon Point is an idyllic white sand beach fringed by swaying palms and flowering plants at the end of a short dirt road for which a small toll is levied, although you can walk round the beach to reach the point. It is Tobago's most famous and most photographed spot, and while access to the beach is free, there is a small charge to use the beachside facilities provided by Pigeon Point Resorts. These include changing rooms, restaurant and bar

Continued on page 84...

Above: Sunset at Pigeon Point, considered as a Caribbean highlight
Below: Pigeon Point pier

Above: Mount Irvine Bay
Below: Mount Irvine Hotel & Sugar Mill Restaurant

where you can sip a rum punch and watch the waves lapping the shore and nearby Buccoo Reef. It is worth popping in to Shore Things, at the nearby Conrado Hotel, which offers a wide range of island arts and crafts at reasonable prices. A number of glass-bottom boats operate from Store Bay and Pigeon Point and tour boats leave here for Buccoo Reef.

Buccoo Reef offers great, safe diving in a marine park off Pigeon Point and is reached by boat from either Pigeon Point or Store Bay. The reef extends for about 10 acres (4 hectares) and because it offers such safe diving, it is the most popular dive site around the island and, as a result, it has over the years, received quite a lot of damage from over-zealous divers. With the current climate of eco-awareness and a policy of leave the coral alone, the reef is, hopefully, now being protected. For non-divers, there are two and a half hour trips in glass-bottomed boats, which include the chance to snorkel over the reef. You also visit the Coral Garden where you can view the spectacularly, multi-hued corals and brilliant tropical fish through the boat's glass bottom. Snorkeling equipment is included in the price of the boat trip ticket.

There are also one day trips including barbecue lunch on **No Man's Land**, a sand spit over the inner reef, with the chance to swim in the **Nylon Pool** a natural shallow pool in the bay which makes a great, naturally heated swimming pool. **Bon Accord Lagoon** is just within Buccoo Reef and offers the best windsurfing on Tobago. More than seventy species of fish have been recorded around the reef including sergeant major, blue tang, grunt, wrasse, doctor, angel and

parrot fish and Harlequin bass, and the area teems with bird life attracted by the crabs, oysters, conch and water snails.

From Crown Point, the old Milford Road runs east through **Bon Accord** and **Canaan**, both settlements with strong links to the Moravian Church. The Moravian missionaries were the first to preach to the slaves. Canaan also has a famous blackboard where local news and gossip can be written up for all to read. There is sometimes horse riding on the firm sands at **Petit Trou Beach** off the Shirvan Road and through the Friendship Estate. Bon Accord Estate switched from sugar cane to coconut production at the beginning of the twentieth century and can be visited. It has many artifacts and pieces of plantation equipment from the eighteenth and nineteenth centuries.

Buccoo Village is most famous for its Sunday night Sunday School, a very lively street party with loud, loud music and lots of singing and dancing, while lovely **Mount Irvine Bay** is noted for its surfing beach and the Mt. Irvine Hotel and championship golf course. One of the hotel's restaurants is built around the old stone sugar mill. It is also a good base if you are interested in sport fishing. Offshore you can find giant blue marlin, both black and white marlin, sailfish, black fin tuna and wahoo. Overlooking the bay at Montgomery is the 1799 Moravian Church, the first on Tobago to bring Christianity to the slaves in the late eighteenth century. The missionaries were often in conflict with the plantation owners because they insisted on bringing education to the slaves as well as religion.

Fairyhaus is the island home and

Grafton Caledonia Wildlife Sanctuary

The Grafton Estate includes the **Grafton Caledonia Wildlife Sanctuary**, which is a delightful place, especially as it arose as a result of a devastating hurricane in 1963, one of the few to hit the island. The estate, a former cocoa plantation, was badly damaged by the storm with hundreds of trees in the surrounding forests uprooted. As the birds' natural habitat was largely destroyed, the owner of the estate started to put food out for them, and the birds started to live much closer to human habitation than normal. When the owner died she left the estate to her family on condition that it remained a nature reserve. The estate house is being converted into a nature center, and birds such as the spectacular insect-eating motmot still emerge from the forest around 4pm, when the old owner used to put out food. Some of the birds will still feed from your hand. There are also several trails into the surrounding forest.

studio of German sculptress Luise Kimme who divides her time between Tobago and Germany. It is in the hills above Mount Irvine and overlooks the settlement, sea and surrounding countryside. She is noted for her impressive works created from huge blocks of wood, mostly large sections of tree trunks hewn locally and aged. From these blocks are sculpted the most magnificent tableaux of dancers, family groups, lovers and figures.

The road then passes Stone Haven Bay and **Turtle Beach**, one of the island's main nesting sites for the giant leatherback turtle. These huge, lumbering but gentle giants come ashore several times between March and July to lay their eggs in the sand. Watching this happen is a magical moment, as it is to see the young hatchlings race for the safety of the sea about three months later. In both cases great care must be taken not to disturb the turtles and it is advisable to go with a guide who can lead you to the best spots –

for both you and the leatherbacks.

Great Courland Bay stretches for about a mile (1.6km) from Black Rock and Fort Bennett to Plymouth. The Dutch started work on the fort in the late 1630s; further fortifications were added by the Courlanders fifty years later, and even more by the British at the beginning of the nineteenth century. The modern Great Courland Bay Monument was designed by sculptor Jons Mintiks and erected in 1978 as a memorial to the original Courlander settlers. Latvians still return to the island for the annual celebrations commemorating their forefathers. Nearby on the Grafton Road is a traditional nineteenth century Moravian Church.

PLYMOUTH

Plymouth was originally called Nieuw Walcheren and was one of the earliest settlements on the island. King James 1 of England ceded the rights of the island to his grandson Jacobus, Duke of Courland; the

Above left & right: Glass bottom boats, Buccoo Reef

Below: Turtle Beach

settlement was founded by Cour-landers (Latvia). During the seven-teenth century, Courland became a major shipbuilding nation and with its strong navy, it attempted to es-tablish an empire. It set up several colonies on Tobago and one on the West African coast in Gambia in 1651. Nieuw Walcheren was founded in 1645 but European wars so weakened Courland that this colony was abandoned after only a year. The **Courland Monument**, that commemorates these pioneer settlers, was sculpted by Janis Mintiks.

Much of the town's development occurred under British military rule which accounts for the ordered, grid layout and the remains of tiny **Fort James** that stands on the headland just west of Portsmouth, and has commanding views as far as Pigeon Point. The fort was originally a barracks built by the British in the early 1760s, and the fortifications that included a series of low walls, cannon and powder house were added a few years later. The former fort gaol is now part

Of interest in the town is an eigh-teenth-century grave known as the **Mystery Tomb** because of its ob-scure inscription. The tomb contains the mortal remains of Betty Stivens who died on 25 November, 1873, and the epitaph on the headstone reads: *She was a mother without knowing it, and a wife without letting her husband know it, except by her kind indulgences to him.* St. David's Parish Church was built in 1825 and was originally the garrison church.

THE NORTH COAST

Just north of Plymouth is Back Bay where traces of early Arawak settlements have been found.

The **Adventure Farm and Nature Reserve** is on the way to Arnos Vale and is worth a stop as you can pick your own fruit from the mango and citrus orchards, and then watch the rich wildlife on the 12-acre (5-hectare) estate. The reserve has many species of birds and butterflies as well as iguanas and other lizards.

At **Arnos Vale** there is the Arnos Vale Hotel incorporating the old estate house, and a small beach and clear waters for snorkeling but care needs to be taken because the waves can be strong. You should also visit the 1857 Glasgow, Scot-land-built **Waterwheel** and other relics and equipment from the sugar estate that was founded in the sixteenth century and operated until the end of the nineteenth cen-tury. There are a number of nature trails in the area, and one of the prettiest runs along the coast from Arnos Vale to Culloden Bay.

The road from Arnos Vale runs inland into the hills to Moriah and nearby **Golden Lane** where you can visit the **Witch's Grave** close to a huge silk cotton tree.

Legend of the witch's grave

According to legend the grave contains the remains of Gang Gang Sara, a witch who flew across the Atlantic from Africa many centuries ago but who lost her magical powers after eating salt. As she was unable to fly home she ended her days on Tobago.

Culloden Bay is a small bay with a horseshoe reef and the **Footprints Eco-Resort,** the first eco-resort on Tobago set in a delightful nature reserve. The 61-acre (24.4-hectare) resort has maximized the use of renewable energy resources in its villas made of local materials. The accommodation is built on columns and the villas are connected by local walkways to minimize ground damage and silt run off. There are nature trails. One of the hills rising above the bay is still known as **Salt Fish Hill** because the catch would be hung out to dry ready for salting.

From Moriah you can drive back to Plymouth via **Les Coteaux** (French for hills and it is easy to see how it got its name) if you want a spectacular drive. The road passes many former plantations including the Franklyn Estate founded by two brothers in the eighteenth century. The Franklyn Village grew up after Emancipation when freed slaves moved in to grow cocoa and coffee.

The road is narrow and twisting as you drive through **Concordia,** an area of hills with deep gorges and dense tropical forests, and it is easy to see why many of the island's myths and folklore are based on this area. Ancestor worship is still common on Tobago and ancestor spirits or Jumbies are said to watch over the land and the people from their vantage points high in the branches of silk cotton trees. If a silk cotton tree has to be cut down for any reason, a bottle of rum has to be offered to the Jumbies in appeasement.

If you have a jeep or four wheel-drive vehicle, you can also head deeper inland towards Mason Hall to see the **Highland Waterfall.**

The area east of Arnos Vale is far less populated than most other parts of the island, and there are fewer facilities for tourists, especially restaurants and filling stations. If exploring this beautiful stretch of coastline, take a picnic lunch and make sure you have a full tank.

From Moriah the road runs to the small fishing village of Castara. A side road takes you to **King Peter Bay** with its black sand and believed to have been named after a Carib ruler. Together with **Cotton Bay** and **Celery Bay,** you have three of the most secluded and beautiful beaches on the island.

This is a very pretty drive with the tree covered hills running down to the coast, waterfalls, and charming little fishing villages set in beautiful bays. **Castara Bay** usually has small fishing boats bobbing in the water while the fishermen repair and dry their nets along the shore. During the night between March and July the sands of the bay become the haunt of nesting leatherback turtles.

Just west of Castara is stunning, sweeping **Englishman's Bay.** It is a much photographed and painted scene, with its crescent of white sands and fringe of coconut trees. There is even a small river running through stands of bamboo to the sea. It is also another important nesting site for the giant leatherback turtles.

Parlatuvier is another of the small fishing villages along this stretch of coast with a small Anglican church looking out to sea, and the fishing boats are anchored in sheltered Parlatuvier Bay.

Bloody Bay was named after a fierce naval battle in the eighteenth century. Some way out from Bloody Bay are the **Sisters Rocks** that offer good snorkeling and scuba diving

FOLKLORE OF TOBAGO

Many spirits are said to roam the land, especially in the dense forests inland. Some of these spirits are benevolent while others are evil and take great pleasure in scaring innocent wayfarers and passers-by. Spirits include:

Papa Bois, also called Daddy Boulchon, is the King of the Woods and often manifests himself as an old man with a long white beard in which leaves are entwined and with cloven hooves instead of feet. He is the protector of the woodlands and the creatures living in them. Those who offend him are led deep into the forest and then abandoned to their fate. If you come across Papa Bois you must treat him with great respect and never look at his feet.

Mama Dlo is the protector of the island's water supplies, and so very important, while **Phantoms** are troll-like creatures who warn of the approach of strangers, and **Soucouyants** are blood-thirsty female vampires.

Lagahoo can appear in many forms, but are often seen in the shape of a wild pig. They suddenly appear late at night and try to frighten people off the road.

Jumbies are benevolent spirits but fierce enemies if annoyed. If offended, they terrorize villages by walking through them late at night dragging a long clanking chain. On their head they carry a coffin filled with bottles of rum and topped by three lit candles.

Dovennes are the spirits of unbaptized children who torment earthly children at dusk and try to lead them into mischief. They are scared off if you circle your home with crushed eggshells.

Obeahs can be both men and women, and they still practise their ancient African beliefs and rituals. They can be called in to exorcise spirits, remove evil spells or cast them and settle disputes. Their skills are inherited so passed down from one generation to the next within the same family.

Because of ancestor worship Tobagonian funerals and wakes are highly ritualized. The deceased is laid out in the coffin in the best room of the house so that all the relatives and friends can visit and pay their last respects. After the funeral service the wake begins and can often last all night and sometimes, several days as the family and other mourners eat and drink while the departed relative's soul passes from one world to the next.

**Above:
Englishman's Bay,
North coast**

**Left: Carnival
member,
Roxborough**

with coral growing on the rocks and a rich marine life including shoals of beautiful angel fish. There is a small church as you descend to Bloody Bay that was built with funds supplied by an Englishman, John Rood, whose wife was killed near the site in a road accident in 1965. For some years the church also doubled as a school.

SOUTH-EAST TO ROXBOROUGH

As you cross the island you drive through the mountains and tropical rain forests. The **Central Ridge** is a mountainous spine that runs the length of the island with deep valleys, small but fast flowing streams and many waterfalls. Many of the waterfalls plunge down into pools where you can take a dip, although the surrounding rocks can be slippery so care needs to be taken. Many of these falls can only be reached by hiking to them, especially King's Bay, Green Hill, Craig Hall and the Pembroke Falls, and, the water flow is obviously much greater during the rainy season.

Children at school in Roxborough

The more accessible and one of the loveliest of these waterfalls is the **Argyle Falls** near Roxborough, although you still need a four-wheel drive vehicle and have to complete the journey on foot. The falls drop over rocks in three cascades surrounded by lush tropical vegetation, and it is possible to climb up along the steep sides of the falls to the top, but it is advisable to use the services of one of the government-trained guides who for a small fee (TT$15) will lead you safely up the least slippery path. They will guide you to the best viewing spots and to where you can cool down under the cascading waters.

The area was declared protected in 1776 the year after Britain took control of the island. You can hike through the **Main Ridge Forest Reserve**, the oldest forest reserve in the Western Hemisphere, and a number of tour operators offer trips along the **Gilpin/Niplig Trail**. The forest area is one of the best bird watching spots on the island and you can see the rare white-tailed sabrewing hummingbird, manakin, trogon, jacobin and chacalaca.

The small town of **Roxborough** looks out over **Prince's Bay**, and you can either turn right and take the Windward Road west back to Scarborough, or head east to explore the north eastern tip of the island including Speyside and Charlotteville. Close to Roxburgh is the **Louis d'Or Nurseries**, worth a visit because of the wide range of flowering trees and fruit trees on display.

THE NORTHERN TIP OF THE ISLAND

The Windward Road north of Roxborough is one of the highlights

of touring Tobago. The road passes **Queen's Bay** and the even more spectacular **King's Bay** with its huge sheltered quay, and the **King's Bay Waterfall**. There are many inland routes that can be explored such as the road along the valley of the Louis d'Or river.

Restaurant in a tree

After King's Bay, the road climbs to **Speyside** where you can dine in a restaurant in a 'tree'. Jemma's Seafood Kitchen is actually built among the branches of an enormous seagrape tree. The restaurant is an island institution and people come from all around to lunch or dine by the water's edge. The menu is simple, usually fish, chicken, lobster or shrimp but the food is fabulous, the portions large and the accompaniments delicious and interesting, especially the breadfruit pie when it is available. There are several other good restaurants in Speyside and most offer great views over Tyrell's Bay across to Little Tobago Island.

Diving attractions in the area include magnificent formations of hard and soft corals, as well as the strong currents that run between the islands. While these particular waters are only suitable for proficient divers, the experience of riding these swift currents has been likened to Superman soaring through the sky. Most dives are within a few minutes' boat ride of Speyside, home

Manta madness

Speyside is the best springboard for enjoying Manta Madness, a phenomenon that can be enjoyed each year between March and July when giant North Atlantic manta rays frequent the area. The rays, which can have wingspans of from 6–15ft (2–4.5m) across – the record is over 30ft (9m) – are friendly and inquisitive, and, according to local dive operators, divers can often 'dance' with these gentle giants who gracefully circle their human 'partners'. The rays frequently approach so close that divers are able to caress the white undersides of the mantas' bodies. At least a dozen mantas frequent the nutrient rich waters around Little Tobago one mile (1.6km) east of Speyside, in an area known as the Cathedral. This is also the home of the world's largest known growth of brain coral that is 12ft (3.6m) high, and 16ft (4.8m) across.

of the new Manta Lodge, and headquarters of the Tobago Dive Experience. The 22-room inn offers seven-night dive packages including accommodation, ten single tank boat dives, airport transfers, taxes and service charges through Scuba Voyages. The company also offers dive packages at the Grafton Beach Resort, a four-star, full service resort on Great Courland Bay, close to Scarborough. The resort's beaches are also popular with leatherback turtles that come ashore at night between March and April to lay their eggs in the sand.

The Coco Reef Resort and Spa, near the Crown Point Airport, also offers a five-day, four-night dive package. It is the island's newest and largest resort with 135 rooms and suites.

From Speyside the road runs across the island through the steep hills and lush forests to **Charlotteville** a small, secluded fishing village lying in a cove in unspoiled **Man O'War Bay** and overlooked by **Fort Cambleton**. It is a lovely,

Birding on Tobago

Apart from its diving, great beaches and relaxed atmosphere, Tobago's other great claim to fame is its bird life, and ornithologists come from around the world to spot the huge number of species. There are parrots that wake you at dawn with their squawking, and the turkey-like Chachalaca, the Tobagonian national bird. Other special species to be seen include blue backed manakin, rufus vented chachalaca, red crowned woodpecker and the white fringed antwren. The best birding area is along the Gilpin Trace where you can see the yellow-legged thrush, blue backed manakin and rare white tailed sabrewing, and many other species.

Charlotteville

Speyside Waterwheel

Little Tobago

This small 450-acre (180-hectare) island lies east of Speyside. The entire island is an important protected nature reserve and is also known as **Bird of Paradise Island**. In 1909, Mr. Ingram, the island's owner, released forty-seven Papua New Guinea birds of paradise. They flourished until 1963 when the island was hit by the devastating hurricane Flora, and the birds of paradise were all killed. The island is still a major Caribbean nesting site, however, for a large number of birds, as well as being an important stopover on the migration routes. You can see colonies of red billed tropicbird, red footed and brown boobies, and sooty and noddy terns. The island is one mile (1.6km) east of Tobago and local fishermen will ferry you across for a fee. The crossing takes about 15 minutes and you can take in a walking tour of the island and enjoy a dive. There are more formal tours at 10am and 2pm that can be arranged through either the Blue Waters Inn or Speyside Inn.

natural anchorage, although it is rarely busy. The anchorage is so large that in 1807 French Admiral Villeneuve hid his fleet here to escape the pursuing Lord Nelson. Each day when the fishing boats return, a conch shell is blown to tell the residents there are fish for sale. Man O'War Bay also includes Lover's Bay and Pirate's Bay (see below). The reef is accessible from Man O'War Bay while inland there are a number of scenic walking trails.

It is possible to drive west along a very rough road past the **Campbelton Battery** built at the start of the nineteenth century, to the village of L'Anse Fourmi but a four-wheel drive vehicle is essential and after heavy rain, the road is often impassable. It is better to re-trace your route and explore the northern coast by taking the cross-island road from Roxburgh to Bloody Bay, or if driving from Scarborough, going anti-clockwise round the island.

From Charlotteville it is a short boat ride across to **St. Giles Island** and **London Bridge**, its natural arch, which offers an exciting *chutre* dive. Also close by are **Marble Island** and the **Fishbowl**, which teem with fish and offer the chance to meet the larger pelagic species attracted by the warm waters and rich feeding. **Pirate's Bay** to the north of Charlotteville gets its name because it was once the haunt of pirates who used it as a base from which to plunder the rich galleons carrying treasures back to England, France, Spain and Holland.

In the most northern point of the island, opposite St. Giles Island is **Flag Staff Hill**, which was the site of a US radio tower and military lookout during the Second World War. There is still a navigational beacon. The views from the summit are breathtaking and you can see quite clearly from the different shades of the water where the Atlantic Ocean and Caribbean Sea meet. The dark blue-black of the Atlantic contrasts with the light green waters of the Caribbean. St Giles Island is an offshore bird sanctuary with many nesting species of seabirds, including a colony of magnificent Frigate birds.

Return to Roxborough and head back along the coast past Prince's Bay and Belle Garden, a former French plantation, to **Richmond Great House**. This is the restored Great House of a former sugar cane plantation. It was built in 1766 and is now a guesthouse with restaurant, although it has a display of African carvings and textiles. There are other Great Houses along this stretch of road such as Kendall between Belle Garden and Rox-burgh, and **Belle Garden House**, originally called Belle Jardin.

At Goldsborough, about 15 minutes inland from Goldsborough Bay, you can visit the **Rainbow Nature Resort and Rainbow Falls**. You should also visit the **Genesis Nature Park and Art Gallery** at Goodwood, the home of local artist Michael Spencer.

Studley Park is the area inland of **Granby Point** and, although there is nothing to show today, it was the site of Georgetown, the island's first capital under British rule from 1763 to 1769. The first sugar exported from the island to England was loaded from Studley Park aboard the Dolly in 1770. And at Granby Point the British built Fort Granby to protect Georgetown and the sea approaches to it. Nothing remains of the fort but if you look around carefully you can spot a single grave, the sole reminder of the area's former occupation. You can get a meal or drink at the Dry Duck Pub and look out at **Smith Island** that lies offshore to the south-east.

It is then a short run back into Scarborough. If you have time, or as a separate trip out, you can turn inland from Studley Park or Barbados Bay – with small **Centipede Island** just offshore, and named because of the large number of rare centipedes found there – to join the Castara Road which runs into the hills and the **Hillsborough Dam** where, if you have a four-wheel drive vehicle, there are lots of opportunities for off the road driving. It is a great area for beautiful scenery, bird watching and hiking. Just after a mile (1.6km) in from the coast you should spot the **Green Hill Waterfall** and there is a short path leading to it.

P l a c e s   t o   V i s i t

TOBAGO

Museum of Tobago History
Fort King George complex, overlooking Scarborough
It is open from Monday to Friday between 9am and 5pm. There is a small admission charge ☎ s639-3970.

Buccoo Reef
Snorkeling equipment is included in the price of the boat trip ticket. Boat trips leave daily from 11am
☎ 639-8519.

Fairyhaus
In the hills above Mount Irvine.
The studio is open on Sunday or by invitation.
☎ 639-0257.

Adventure Farm and Nature Reserve
On the way to Arnos Vale.
It is open Monday to Friday from 7am to 5pm and guided tours are available. There is a small admission price.
☎ 639-2839.

Arnos Vale Waterwheel and Nature Park
Open daily.
☎ 639-2881.

Louis d'Or Nurseries
Close to Roxburgh
Open daily and admission is free.
☎ 660-4329.

Richmond Great House.
There are guided tours of the house
☎ 660-4467.

$ inexpensive
$$ moderate
$$$ expensive

Arnos Vale Waterwheel $$
Franklyn Road
☎ 660-0815
European and Caribbean cuisine.

Arthur's By The Sea $$
Milford Road, Crown Point
☎ 639-0196
Creole and seafood.

Baynes Seafood House $$
Post Office Street, Buccoo
☎ 639-9705
Seafood.

Bayside $$
Crown Point
☎ 639-0196
Local and international.

Le Beau Rivage $-$$
Mount Irvine Bay Hotel Golf Club
☎ 639-8871
A beautiful setting for lovely food featuring French and Caribbean cuisine with an impressive list of French wines.

Best of Thymes $$
Ocean Point, Lowlands
☎ 639-0207
A cosy restaurant in a garden setting with à la carte menu and specializing in seafood, local cuisine, East Indian dishes, and grills. It is open for breakfast and dinner.

Blue Crab Restaurant $$-$$$
Main Street
☎ 639-2737
An island institution serving traditional Creole cuisine and fresh fruit and vegetables, often from the garden. Dinner reservations recommended.

Creole food at Speyside

Jemma's in Tree Restaurant, Speyside

Blue Haven $$
Bacolet Bay
☎ 660-7400
International.

Bonkers $$
Toucan Inn, Crown Point
☎ 639-7173
A really fun place every evening
attracting locals and islanders alike.
Open daily from 8am until late with
good value local and international
cuisine and live entertainment most
nights. Great breakfasts and try the
house specialty, passion fruit juice
pressed from fruit grown around the
pool.

Bougainvillea $$
Studley Park
☎ 660-2075
Creole and seafood.

Café Petunia $
Old Milford Road
☎ 639-6970
Salads and snacks.

Carat Shed $$
Old Milford Road, Hamden
☎ 639-7522
Local cuisine and seafood.

Cocoa House $$
Footprints
☎ 660-0118
Local dishes.

Cocrico Inn $$
North Street, Plymouth
☎ 639-2961
Island dishes.

Cuffie River $$
Runnemede
☎ 660-0505
Local and Creole.

Dillon's $$
Crown Point
☎ 639-8765
Great seafood, and open daily except Monday for dinner from 6pm. Reservations recommended.

Eleven Degrees North $$
Store Bay Road
☎ 639-0996
An interesting establishment that combines a restaurant and art gallery with new world cuisine. It is open from Tuesday to Saturday.

Emerald $$
Stone Haven Bay
☎ 639-0539
Renowned for its lobsters. Traditional island fare in a charming setting.

Fishpot $$
Blue Waters Inn
☎ 660-2583
Local dishes and seafood.

Garden Grill $$
Ocean Point
☎ 639-7842
Local and international.

Grafton Beach Resort $$$
Black Rock
☎ 639-0191
Seafood, local and international dishes. Excellent seafood.

Indigo $$
Pleasant Prospect
☎ 639-9635
Island dishes.

Jacaranda $$$
Mount Irvine Bay Hotel
Mount Irvine Bay
☎ 639-8871
An extensive à la carte menu with local and international dishes in an elegant setting with attentive service.

Jaff's Harbour Wok $$
Milford Road, Scarborough
☎ 639-2745
Oriental and seafood dishes with take away.

Jemma's Sea View Kitchen $$
Speyside
☎ 660-4066
Great fish and seafood in a fantastic setting overooking the water. A must.

Kariwak Village Restaurant $$
Store Bat Road, Crown Point
☎ 639-8442
Caribbean cuisine and island dishes.

Leandros $$
Le Grand Courlan, Black Rock
☎ 639-9667
Seafood, pasta and Mediterranean dishes. Pizzas, hot dogs, burgers, cakes and pastries.

Man Friday $$-$$$
Sandy Point Beach Club, Crown Point
☎ 639-9547
Great waterfront dining with international cuisine and Thai dishes.

Me Shells $$
Shirvan and Buccoo Roads
☎ 631-0353
International and local cuisine.

Neptune's $$
Grafton Beach Resort
☎ 639-0191
Local and seafood.

Ocean View $$
Grafton Beach Resort
☎ 639-0191
Mexican/Italian/Chinese mix.

Old Donkey Cart $$
Windward Road
☎ 639-3551
Creole and island dishes.

Patino's $$-$$$
Enchanted Waters,
☎ 639-9481
Seafood, Caribbean and Polynesian
menu.

Rouselle's $$-$$$
Old Windward Road, Bacolet
☎ 639-4738
A great place for dining and liming
every night except Sunday with
lovely seafood and exotic local
cuisine with a difference.

The SeaHorse Inn $$-$$$
Old Grafton Road, Blackrock
☎ 639-0686
A lovely beachside setting offering
patio or balcony dining, great
sunsets, seafood, steaks, Creole and
international cuisine.

Shirran Watermill $$-$$$
Mount Pleasant
☎ 639-0000
Seafood and steaks in an elegant
outdoor setting.

Steak and Lobster Grill $$
Sandy Point
☎ 639-8533
Seafront dining with fresh fish,
seafood and prime US steaks.

Stonehaven $$
Bon Accord
☎ 639-0102
International.

The Sugar Mill $$-$$$
Mount Irvine Bay Hotel
Mount Irvine Bay
☎ 639-8871
Elegant gourmet French and
nouvelle Creole dining in the
beautifully restored seventeenth-
century sugar mill built with hand
hewn blocks of island coral stone.

Sunset Grill $$
Crown Point
☎ 639-8512
International and local dishes.

La Tartaruga$$
Buccoo Bay
☎ 639-0940
Restaurant specializes in seafood and
Italian dishes with home made pasta
and pizza and a café bar.

Village Restaurant $$
Kariwak Village, Crown Point
☎ 639-8545
Caribbean dishes. Reservations
recommended.

NIGHTLIFE

Most of the nightlife is concentrated
on the resort hotels, especially those
around Store Bay. The Grafton Beach
Resort has nightly entertainment, as
does Le Grand Courlan. Local folk
troops such as Black Rock and Les
Couteaux are really good and
regularly appear at the various
hotels. There is The Deep, Sandy
Point Hotel's disco, and lively Pat's
Place, on the outskirts of
Scarborough, which never seems to
close and offers good Creole food.
There is live jazz at the Peacock Mill
at Canaan, and there is the weekly
jump up on Sundays in Buccoo
Village. Also try Bonkers, Columbus
Bar and the Golden Star, all at
Crown Point, and the Starting Gate
on the Shirvan Road.

Accommodation & Sports Facilities

3

Speyside Inn Restaurant & beach

The islands have a wide range of accommodation to suit all tastes and pockets, from the five star all-inclusive resorts to inns, and modest but friendly, family run guesthouses, self-catering apartments and beach cottages.

All-inclusive resorts are just that, the price covers everything including drinks and all facilities. The service is first class and prices reflect this.

If you want to eat out and explore quite a lot, it may pay to stay in a hotel offering part board, or one of the many inns on the island, some of them converted plantation homes, and generally offering excellent value for money.

There are also apartments, holiday villas and beach cottages available for rent offering you the privacy of your own accommodation and the flexibility to eat in or out.

The following is not a complete list of accommodation available but it is comprehensive and includes a good selection of properties in all price categories.

Prices: guide prices are winter rates for single occupancy and are exclusive of the 10% Hotel Room Tax. Summer rates are usually lower. $ represents inexpensive accommodation, $$ moderate, and $$$ deluxe.

The Hotel and Tourism Association is at:

The Travel Centre, Uptown Mall, 44058 Edward Street, Port of Spain ☎ 624-3928.

HOTELS

TRINIDAD

Abercromby Inn $-$$
Abercromby Street, Port of Spain
☎ 623-5259
The inn is conveniently located in downtown and has 8 deluxe rooms and 8 economy rooms, all self contained. Car rentals are available. It is a good overnight stop if you are catching the early Tobago ferry.

Asa Wright Nature Centre $$$
Blanchisseuse Road, Arima
☎ 667-4655
A really get away from it all place and perfect if you like nature and wildlife. There are 26 rooms in the main lodge and cabanas, set in the 200 acre (80 hectares) nature reserve at 1,200ft (366m) above sea level in the tropical rain forest. There is a dining room serving tasty buffet meals using home grown fruit, vegetables and coffee, nature trails, field trips and a fabulous verandah where you can sit and enjoy the incredible views and watch the prolific bird life just feet away.

**Bel Air International
Airport Hotel $$**
Piarco International Airport, Piarco
☎ 664-4771
The hotel is three minutes from the airport and ideal for stopovers, early departures or late arrivals with 24-hour courtesy service to and from the terminal. It has 56 rooms, including 8 family rooms and 14 poolside rooms. There is a restaurant, cocktail party and pool, and there is a special barbecue dinner with live entertainment every Saturday.

Carnetta's Inn $
Saddle Road, Maraval

☎ 628-2732
Small good value property with 14 rooms.

Chaconia Inn $$
106 Saddle Road, Maraval
☎ 628-8603
Nestling in the Maraval Valley, yet only five minutes from downtown Port of Spain, the inn offers 31 newly refurbished suites and 6 deluxe rooms with kitchenettes. The Dining Room offers local and European specialties, or you can dine al fresco in the Roof Garden Restaurant. There is a pool, and live nightly entertainment and dancing, with nearby bathing, golf and tennis.

Coral Cove Marina Hotel $$
Western Main Road, Chaguaramas
☎ 634-2040
A 14-room resort hotel with restaurant, bar, beach and watersports.

CrewsInn and Marina $$
Chaguaramas Terminals Drive
☎ 634-4384
New property with 46 rooms, restaurant, bar and full service marina.

Holiday Inn Hotel $$-$$$
Wrightson Road, Port of Spain
☎ 625-3366 and 1-800-HOLIDAY
In the heart of the capital with 235 newly renovated rooms, and exotic dining in La Ronde, the Caribbean's only revolving restaurant. There is a fully equipped business section, conference rooms, fitness facilities and pool with sunken bar.

Hosanna Hotel $-$$
2 Santa Margarita Circular Road, St. Augustine
☎ 662-5449
A Christian hotel offering good accommodation in 19 large rooms with restaurant, pool, conference

facilities and 24-hour gospel music in the rooms for those who want it.

Hotel Esterol $$
Cumana Toco
☎ 662-4084
Luxurious French villa and spa with luxury suites, restaurant, bar and pool.

Kapok Hotel $$
16-18 Cotton Hill, St. Clair
☎ 622-5765
This charming, comfortable hotel sits at the foot of Cotton Hill and within easy walking distance of downtown Port of Spain. There are 94 large rooms, suites and studios with kitchenette facilities. The Kapok boasts two of Port of Spain's finest restaurants, Tiki Village and Café Savanna. Tiki Village offers rooftop views of Port of Spain and excellent Chinese and Polynesian cuisine, while the Café Savanna is noted for its refined Caribbean menu. There are also secretarial services and conference and meeting facilities.

Laguna Mar Nature Estates $-$$
Paria Main Road, Blanchisseuse
☎ 628-3731
A small beachfront property with 16 rooms in villas and the main house, set in a nature reserve, with restaurant, sandy beach and swimming lagoon.

Monique's Guesthouse $-$$
114 Saddle Road, Maraval
☎ 628-3334
A friendly and welcoming guest house cum motel with large and very comfortable 19 en-suite rooms set in the attractive gardens. The location is convenient for all the attractions of Maraval and downtown Port of Spain. There is a dining room serving breakfast, dinners are available.

Mount Plaisir Estate Hotel $$
Grand Riviere
☎ 670-8381
A small, comfortable 10-room hotel close to the beach with meeting rooms.

Normandie Hotel $$
10 Nook Avenue, St. Anns
☎ 624-1181
The elegant property, founded by French Creole owners in the 1930s, is in a valley flanked by the Botanical Gardens on the edges of the lush tropical rain forest yet is within easy walking distance of the heart of Port of Spain. The restaurant is named after the old plantation, La Fantasie, and features Cuisine Creole Nouvelle, a blend of local dishes and new trends in French food. The hotel stands on the site of the old great house. The hotel has its own piazza, Café Trinidad, market and art gallery featuring paintings and sculptures by island artists. The recently refurbished and upgraded property has 53 spacious rooms and loft apartments are set around the courtyard with swimming pool.

Ocean Point $
Milford Road, Lowlands
☎ 639-0973
There are 10 ocean view apartments with fully equipped kitchens and private balconies, pool, barbecue pits, poolside dining area and cocktail bar. The Best of Thymes Restaurant offers à la carte dining and East Indian dishes.

Pelican Inn Resorts $
2-4 Coblentz Avenue, Cascade
☎ 627-6271
Good value, friendly inn with 20 comfortable rooms, with restaurant, pub and squash courts.

Royal Hotel $$
46-54 Royal Road, San Fernando
☎ 652-4881

A 60-room property with kitchenettes available. There are also meeting facilities.

Royal Palm Suite Hotel $$
7 Saddle Road, Maraval
☎ 628-5086
The hotel, in the heart of Maraval, boasts 70 of the largest rooms, suites and executive suites in the Caribbean, all with fully fitted kitchenettes. There is the Buccaneer's Cove Restaurant and bar specializing in Caribbean cuisine, the Arabic Ali Baba Restaurant, A Pang Chinese Restaurant and Maharani's Indian Restaurant. The complex also contains pool, 16 gift shops, a pharmacy, laundry, dry cleaners, bookshop and disco with nightly entertainment. Tours can be arranged, and it also has secretarial services and conference and meeting facilities. Close to tennis, golf, gym and horseback riding.

Tradewinds Hotel $-$$
38 London Street, St. Joseph Village, San Fernando
☎ 652-9463
There are 16 rooms with kitchen facilities.

Trinidad Hilton Hotel $$$
Port of Spain
☎ 624-3211
This luxury property is in 25 acres (10 hectares) of tropical grounds one mile (1.6km) from Port of Spain and bounded by the Northern Range, the Gulf of Paria and Queen's Park Savannah. There are 394 spacious rooms and suite combinations, each with their own balcony; two executive floors and wheel chair accessible guest rooms. The hotel is known locally as the 'upside down hotel' as it is built on the hillside and the reception near the top of the hill so the floor numbers increase as you descend. The La Boucan Restaurant offers fine dining with International

and West Indian cuisine, and live entertainment during afternoon tea and dinner. There are several bars, including the late night Carnival Bar and the Lobby Bar that serves snacks and drinks overnight. Facilities include pool, table tennis and floodlit tennis, badminton, theme party evenings and activities schedule, business and secretarial services and several function rooms.

Trinidad Maracas Bay Hotel $$
Maracas Bay
☎ 669-1643
A new property with 40 rooms by the beach with restaurant, bar and pool.

Tropical Hotel $-$$
Rookery Nook, Maraval
☎ 622-5815
It has 15 comfortable rooms and offers a seafood restaurant open daily for lunch and dinner, the Bamboo Room Night Club and pool.

Valley Vue Hotel $$
67 Ariapita Road, St. Anns
☎ 624-0940
There are 68 rooms with facilities for the disabled, swimming pool, gym, sauna and aerobics center, squash and tennis, live entertainment, grand ballroom, and conference and meeting facilities.

Villa Maria Inn $
48a Perseverence Road, Haleland Park, Maraval
☎ 629-8023
Close to Maracas Bay and Port of Spain and set in a lush tropical valley, the 15-room inn offers rooms sleeping one to four. There is a pool.

Vista del Mar $$
Western Industrial Estate, Trincity
☎ 663-2394

TOBAGO

Adventure Eco-Villas $$
Arnos Vale Road, Plymouth
☎ 639-2839

Small property set on an adventure farm and nature reserve.

Arnos Vale Hotel $$-$$$
Vale Road, Plymouth
☎ 660-2881
Built among a 400 acre (165 hectare) former sugar plantation with 29 rooms set in beautiful grounds, the old Manor House now contains the restaurant, bar, reception and lounge. Afternoon tea is served on the verandah and the birds assemble to watch and take advantage of crumbs. The rooms are in cottages set in the gardens or near the beach. There is a pool and swim up bar, beach restaurant, tennis, golf, scuba and snorkeling, fishing, sailing and sightseeing with evening entertainment.

Arthur's By The Sea $$
Milford Road, Crown Point
☎ 639-0196
There are 20 new, comfortable rooms each with private patio, an open-air full service restaurant and cocktail bar, large guest lounge, pool and souvenir and gift shop. It is close to fine beaches and a short walk from Store Bay and Pigeon Point Resort, and a 15-minute drive from Scarborough. Activities which can be arranged include snorkeling, Buccoo Reef trips, tennis, scuba, bird watching, golf, sailing, nature tours, deep sea fishing, windsurfing, and cycle, scooter and car rentals and nearby duty free shopping.

Bellevista Apartments $-$$
Sandy Point
☎ 639-9351
There are 20 self-contained apartments with private balconies overlooking the sea, with swimming pool and close to Store Bay and Pigeon Point.

Blue Haven $-$$
Bacolet Bay
☎ 660-7400
A delightful blend of old and new with 55 rooms in a newly refurbished historic inn. Solar water heating and fitness suite.

Blue Waters Inn $$-$$$
Batteaux Bay, Speyside
☎ 660-4341
The inn has 32 guest rooms including bungalows, suites and efficiencies, close to the blue waters of the Atlantic, and a little off the main tourist beat, set in 46 acres (18 hectares) of tropical gardens and tucked away in its own private bay. It offers seclusion and tranquility, and the waterfront restaurant that specializes in local dishes and seafood. It is a great base for those who want to laze on the beach, dive or go nature watching. It has a PADI dive center run by Aquamarine Dive. Activities include tennis, nearby golf, scuba, snorkeling, glass bottom boat trips, kayaking, deep-sea fishing, windsurfing and trips to Little Tobago Island.

Bougainvillea Inn $
Studley Park
☎ 660-2075
Lying half way between the airport and Charlotteville on the windward coast, the inn with rooms and apartments overlooks the ocean and is an ideal retreat for nature lovers and bird watchers. There is a dining room and the bar is noted for its wine list.

Opposite page; Top: The Speyside Inn Bottom: Blue Waters Inn, Speyside

Cholson Chalets $
Man O'War Bay
☎ 639-8553
Pleasant budget property with
17 beachside rooms.

Coco Reef Resort $$$
Coconut Bay
☎ 639-8571
The island's newest and largest
property with 135 luxury rooms,
suites and villas. The designers were
asked to incorporate Trinidad's
eclectic architecture and to make
the property look and feel Caribbean,
which they certainly achieved in this
magnificent building with its
columned *porte-cochère* and long
winding palm-lined driveway though
the 10-acre tropical gardens.

The hotel includes a number of
environmentally friendly features,
such as extensive use of recycled
materials and the exclusive use of
island softwoods. The resort is set in
10 acres (4 hectares) of landscaped
gardens by three of Tobago's most
beautiful beaches – Store Bay,
Pigeon Point and Coconut Beach –
and a five-minute drive from Crown
Point International Airport. Rooms
feature tiled patios and balconies,
wall stencils and hand crafted wicker
furniture, and facilities include
swimming pool, championship
floodlit tennis courts and club,
health club and spa, nearby golf,
sailing, water skiing, scuba and
snorkeling, windsurfing, deep sea
fishing and horse back riding, as well
as daily activities schedule, shopping
arcade, beauty salon, car rentals, and
more than 3,000sq.ft of meeting
space. It offers honeymoon packages
and there is a special Lover's
Cottage. Tamara's offers interna-
tional dining based on the freshest of
local ingredients in an elegant but
casual atmosphere. Bacchanals is a

more casual restaurant and bar on
the beach serving lunch and snacks
during the day, and Caribbean
cuisine under the stars in the
evening. Bobsters is an intimate
Champagne Bar, and you can enjoy a
Caribbean cocktail or afternoon tea
in The Gallery Bar and Lounge.

Coconut Inn $-$$
Store Bay
☎ 639-8493
Property combining B&B chalets and
guesthouse facilities with 38 rooms.

Conrado Beach Resort $-$$
Milford Extension Road, Pigeon
Point
☎ 639-9351
The two-floor 31-room property is
right on the beach at Pigeon Point
set in very quiet surroundings, with
restaurant and bar.

Crown Point Beach Hotel $$
Crown Point
☎ 639-8781
Set in 7 acres (2.8 hectares) of
landscaped gardens on Store Bay
with 90 rooms, some with kitchen-
ettes. There is a pool, tennis and
meeting facilities.

Cuffie River Nature Retreat $$
Runnemede
☎ 660-0505
Small 10-room property set amid
lush vegetation ideal for hiking,
birding and nature study.

Enchanted Waters $$
Shirvan Road, Buccoo
☎ 639-9481
Family owned 10-room hotel with
pool, waterfall and courtyard café.

Footprints Eco Resort $$-$$$
Culloden Bay
☎ 660-0118
Set in a 61-acre (24.5-hectare)
nature reserve with the Culloden
Reef just offshore, this was Tobago's
first eco-resort built from local

materials, incorporating renewable energy resources, purification plants and aiming at total self sufficiency in fruits, vegetables and herbs. The accommodation is in studio units and thatched-roof, wooden, one and two bedroom villas that blend in with the scenery. The cabins, with solar powered heating, appliances and jacuzzi, are built on columns and connected by boardwalks to minimize ground damage. Each villa also features the work of a local artist. There is also a honeymoon cottage, fitness suite, library, boutique, restaurant and bar plus nature trails for bird watching, jogging and hiking, the reef for scuba and snorkeling.

Grafton Beach Resort $$$
Black Rock
☎ 639-0191
Set in 5 acres (2 hectares) of lovely gardens in a palm-fringed bay, the resort offers high levels of comfort and service. There are 98 cheerful rooms and 2 deluxe suites with private jacuzzi. You can dine in or out, dance much of the night away and take advantage of the activities schedule. Facilities include pool and swim up bar, beach with bar, air-conditioned squash courts, gym, shuffle board, dive shop, and a wide range of water sports. There is nearby golf and the resort has its own shops, beauty salon and car rental service. There are also extensive conference facilities.

Great Plantation House Hotel $$$
see Sanctuary Villa Resort.

Hilton Tobago $$$
Lowlands
☎ 1 800 HILTON
Situated within the Sanctuary Villa Resort, a luxury hotel with 200 rooms and suites, restaurants, bars, shops, pool set in 60 acres (24 hectares) with children's learning

facility, glass-bottom boats, watersports, diving and nature hikes.

Jimmy's Holiday Resort $-$$
Scarborough
☎ 639-8292
There are 18 self-contained, two-bedroom resorts, close to the beach, airport and restaurants. There is a mini-mart on the property.

Kariwak Village $$
Crown Point
☎ 639-8442
This small 20-room property is noted for its friendliness and its acclaimed Village Restaurant that serves the best of traditional Caribbean cuisine. It is close to the airport and a short walk from the beaches. The rooms are in ten cabanas set around the pool and surrounded by lush tropical vegetation. There is live music at weekends.

Le Grand Courland $$$
Black Rock
☎ 639-9667
This new property has 78 luxury oceanfront rooms and suites and is on the island's leeward coast, 15 minutes north of Scarborough and five miles (8km) from the airport. It stands on a long stretch of wide, sandy beach with a gentle hillside draped with bougainvillea, frangipani and hibiscus behind. Rooms feature custom-made furniture of Trinidadian teak, Italian porcelain floor tiles, and are decorated with original island paintings and batiks, and garden rooms have a private hot tub on a private patio. The restaurant offers an international à la carte menu. There is a Mediterranean Bistro, health food bar, nightly entertainment, duty free shop and boutiques.
 Sports facilities include a large pool with swim up bar, spa facility with sauna, beauty treatment salon,

masseurs, health bar, dive shop, indoor squash, floodlit tennis, nearby golf and a wide range of watersports including diving. There is also a reading lounge, business facility and boardroom available for meetings. It offers a number of packages including Honeymooners' Dream, Tropical Rainfall Adventure and Deep Sea Fishing Adventure, as well as island tours and car rental.

Mt. Irvine Bay Hotel and Golf Resort $$$
Mt. Irvine
☎ 639-8871
Set amid an old sugar and coconut plantation and overlooking the Caribbean, the hotel offers a luxurious, hideaway for those who want to be pampered. There are 105 refurbished superior rooms and luxury suites in the main building, with twin and double spacious Garden Cottage rooms scattered through the 16 acres (6.4 hectares) of tropical gardens. All rooms have balcony or patio and local crafted mahogany furniture. There is a choice of restaurants from the Sugar Mill, in the 200-year old mill at the heart of the estate, the elegant Le Beau Rivage gourmet restaurant in the original golf clubhouse overlooking the 18th green, and the à la carte Jacaranda, plus five bars. Facilities include a large pool with swim up bar, palm-fringed beach with changing facilities, snacks and drinks, and regular entertainment. The 18-hole championship 72-par golf course is next to the hotel and is considered one of the finest in the Caribbean. There are two floodlit tennis courts, and horse riding plus watersports including scuba, snorkeling, windsurfing, water skiing, hydrosliding, hobie cat

sailing and fishing. There are also extensive conference, meeting and banqueting facilities.

Plantation Beach Villas $$
Stonehaven Bay, Blackrock
☎ 639-9377
There are six luxurious two floor, three bedroom villas furnished in Colonial style and decorated with traditional West Indian gingerbread fretwork and large airy verandahs, set among trees overlooking the pool and bay and its long palm-fringed beach. Maid service is provided. The property is next to a bird sanctuary and close to championship golf, restaurants and other attractions.

Rex Turtle Beach Resort $$$
Courland Bay
☎ 639-2851
This luxury resort offers 125 rooms set in two and three floor buildings amid landscaped tropical gardens along a lovely palm-fringed beach. Restaurants include the Kiskadee offering à la carte and table d'hôte menus and theme nights, and the more casual Courlanders coffee shop. There are several bars, large pool, beach and live entertainment most nights. Activities include windsurfing, sunfish sailing, snorkeling, shuffle board and beach volley ball, floodlit tennis, water skiing and watersports tuition, scuba diving and deep sea fishing, with nearby golf. The resort has a shop, business and secretarial services, and meeting and conference facilities.

Richmond Great House $$
Belle Garden
☎ 660-4467
The late eighteenth-century house sits in tropical gardens on a hilltop with views over the rain forests and the sea, and makes a great base for touring the island or just relaxing. The carefully restored house contains many pieces of antique

Plantation Villas

furniture and is owned by a Tobago-born professor of African history whose art collection is displayed. There are 10 rooms and suites, and the dining room serves home grown food and freshly baked bread. There is a pool and outside bar with some beautiful, secluded beaches within walking distance.

Sanctuary Villa Resort $$$
Grafton Estate
☎ 639-9556
Tobago's newest luxury villa resort and hotel complex. Situated on 21 acres of undulating land, surrounded by over 260 acres of wildlife and nature reserve, with truly spectacular views of lush greenery, the famous Buccoo Reef and Caribbean Sea. Luxury one to four bedroom villas with pools are scattered through the grounds and the Plantation Great House Hotel (due to open late 2001) with 22 rooms and suites and a further 28 hillside rooms is being developed. There are restaurants, bars, health club, spa, waterpark and dive facility.

Stonehaven Villas $$-$$$
Grafton Estate
☎ 639-0102
Luxury 3-bedroom villas with private pool and personal housekeeper.

Tobago Plantations $$$
Lowlands
☎ 639-8000
This vast, eco-sensitive luxury resort offers a unique combination of natural and built amenities. Along the 2.5 miles (4km) of coastline, the villa and hotel resort offers nature trails through virgin mangrove forest, championship golf, watersports, walking and jogging trails, gym, spa, tennis and nature tours.

A 120-berth Marina and Yacht Club, a Bird Sanctuary, and a Resort Village with shopping and entertainment complex are planned. When completed the resort will comprise three hotels, the first already open is the Tobago Hilton, as well as 74 luxury condominiums, 57 spacious villas, 61 bungalows and golf and Country Club House with Golf Academy.

Toucan Inn $-$$
Store Bay Local Rod, Crown Point
☎ 639-7173
An imaginative, attractive property with 10 rooms in all-teak cabanas set around the pool. Lively Bonkers restaurant and bar, sun deck, gardens, mini-aviary, entertainment most nights and it is close to the beach.

Tropikist Beach Hotel $$
Crown Point
☎ 639-8512
Set in 5 acres (2 hectares) of landscaped gardens with 33 deluxe rooms, all with sea views, restaurants, pools, pool bar, disco, sports, watersports and dive facility.

Woodlands Estate Nature Resort $$
Woodlands Estate
☎ 639-6816
Set in 100 acres (40 hectares) of unspoiled land on the leeward side of Main Ridge. This 40-room property is an ideal base for hiking, birding, nature trails and horse riding. There is outdoor dining, bar and conference facility.

THERE ARE SEVERAL CHARMING AND INEXPENSIVE GUESTHOUSES:

Trinidad

Airport View Guesthouse $
St. Helena Junction, Piarco
☎ 664-3186

Alicia's Guesthouse $
7 Coblentz Gardens, St. Ann's
☎ 623-2802/8651

Fabienne's Guesthouse $
15 Belle Smythe Street, Woodbrook
☎ 622-2773

Five Star Guesthouse $
7 French Street, Woodbrook
☎ 623-4006

Halyconia Inn $
7 Ist Avenue, Cascade
☎ 623-0008

Jireh's Guesthouse $
109 Long Circular Road, Marava
☎ 628-2337

Mikanne Hotel $
14 Railway Avenue, Plaisance Park, Point-a-Pierre
☎ 659-2584

Naden's Court Guesthouse $
32 St. Augustine Circular Road, Tunapuna
☎ 645-2937

Par-May-La's Inn $
53 Picton Street, Port of Spain
☎ 628-2008

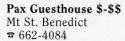

Pax Guesthouse $-$$
Mt St. Benedict
☎ 662-4084

Tobago

Arcadia Nature Resort $$
Orange Hill
☎ 639-1246

Coral Inn Guesthouse $
Store Bay Local Road
☎ 639-0967

Green Acres Hotel Inn $
Cambee
☎ 639-8287

Hampden Inn $
Milford Road, Hampden
☎639-7522

Serenity Apartments $
Centre Street, Canaan
☎ 639-0753

BED AND BREAKFAST PROPERTIES

Bed and breakfast properties offer the chance to spend time in a typical island home, and are not required to charge either room tax or VAT.

Trinidad

St. Ann's, Cascade and Maraval areas:

Cascade Cottage, 16 Second Avenue, Cascade ☎ 623-4481

The Gardens, 15 St. Ann's Avenue, St. Ann's ☎ 625-7692

Gemma's, Pole 86-87 Ariapita Road, St. Ann's ☎ 624-4044

Green Mt. Lodge, Pole 90, Ariapita Road, St. Ann's ☎ 625-3773

Ivis, 12 Fondes Amandes, St. Ann's ☎ 624-3276

Jeanette Price, 5 Sunny Place, Cascade ☎ 623-6605

The Morgan's,
48 Perseverence Road,
Haleland Park, Maraval
☎ 629-2587

Mountain View, 14 Eckel Avenue, Maraval ☎ 622-1962

Scott's Bed and Breakfast,
5a Pomme Rose Avenue, Cascade
☎ 624-4105

Zollna House, 12 Ramlogan Development, Maraval ☎ 628-3731

Belmont, Woodbrook and Newtown areas:

Ana Villa, 5 Ana Street, Woodbrook ☎ 627-2563

Harper's House, 38 Cornelio Street, Woodbrook ☎ 628-0717

Johnson's, 16 Buller Street, Woodbrook ☎ 628-7553

June's, 36 Belmont Valley Road, Belmont ☎ 624-0258

Kitty's, 26 Warren Street, Woodbrook ☎ 622-2567

The Little Inn, 41 Picton Street, New Town ☎ 628-4034

ML's, 25 Stone Street, Woodbrook ☎ 625-3663

Petra Villa, 74 Petra Street, Woodbrook ☎ 622-4988

Rita's Self Catering, 18 de Verteuil Street, Woodbrook ☎ 627-6308

Villa Marigold, 1a Farrell Lane, Belmont ☎ 624-1922

Port of Spain:

Allison's Bed and Breakfast,
30 Victoria Square South, Duke Street ☎ 625-1975

Cornetto's House, 28 Scotland Terrace, Andalusia, Maraval
☎ 628-2732

May's, 35 Victoria Square South, Duke Street ☎ 625-1975

St. Clair and St. James area:

Alcazar House, 13 Alcazar House, St. Clair ☎ 628-8612

Anesta's, 16 Gray Street, St. Clair ☎ 622-5409

La Maison Rustique, 16 Rust Street, St. Clair ☎ 622-1512

Marcelle's, 38 Carlton Avenue, St. James ☎ 622-4575

Trini House, 5a Lucknow Street, St. James ☎ 628-7550

Zeeta's, 10 St. James Terrace, St. James ☎ 622-7165

Blanchisseuse:

Second Spring, 67.75 Mile Post, Paria Main Road ☎ 669-3909

Surf's Country Inn, Pole 197, Lower Village, North Coast Road ☎ 669-2475

Diego Martin and Petit Valley areas:

Ansong, 1 Sapphire Drive, Diamond Vale, Diego Martin ☎ 637-4516

Brendalyn Metz, 15 Dorchester Walk, Petit Valley ☎ 637-1136

Caribbean Condo Villas, 40 Majuba Cross Road, Petit Valley ☎ 632-0113

Carolyn's, 10 Unity Gardens, Rich Plain, Diego Martin ☎ 632-2194

Cecil's, 16 Sapphire Crescent, Diamond Vale, Diego Martin ☎ 637-9329

Chez Moi, 3 Margaret Avenue, Diego Martin ☎ 637-4181

Hillvue Bed and Breakfast, Pole 51, St. Lucien Road, Diego Martin ☎ 632-8046

La Grande Maison, 29 Sapphire Drive, Diamond Vale, Diego Martin ☎ 637-7251

Lin's Bed and Breakfast, 8 Diamond Boulevard, Diamond Vale, Diego Martin ☎ 637-9680

Morgan's Bed and Breakfast, Mountain View Drive, Petit Valley ☎ 633-1188

Seal's, 8 Road Reserve, La Estancia Drive, Diego Martin ☎ 637-1005

Teresita's, 20 Pearle Gardens, Petit Valley ☎ 637-6397

Tacarigua, Trincity, Arouca and El Dorado area:

Parklane Bed and Breakfast, Parklane Court, Amethyst Drive, El Dorado ☎ 663-5265

Sadila House, 3 Waterpipe Road, Arouca ☎ 640-3659

D'Abadie and Arima area:

Kennedy's, 16 Berthe Street, Arima ☎ 667-7148

The Red House, 20 Pinto Road, Santa Rosa Heights ☎ 667-4151

Westmoorings, Glencoe and Carenage area:

A & J Bed and Breakfast, 8 Sanora Park, Point Cumana ☎ 632-4313

Flambeau Colony Bed and Breakfast, 37 Newberry Hill Extension, Glenco ☎ 637-9548

Wellington Inn, 47a Gairlock Road, Glencoe ☎ 632-4472

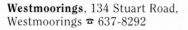

Westmoorings, 134 Stuart Road,
Westmoorings ☎ 637-8292

St. Joseph, St. Augustine and Valsayn area:

La Belle Maison, 108a Valley View,
Maracas, St. Joseph ☎ 663-4413

Casablanca, 3 Prima Road,
Valsayn South, Valsayn ☎ 663-3863

Loira Villa, 31 Ashland Avenue,
Valsayn North, Valsayn ☎ 662-5682

Norma's Bed and Breakfast,
2 Arauc Road, Valsayn South,
Valsayn ☎ 663-4137

Valsayn Villa, 34 Gilwell Road,
Valsayn North ☎ 645-1193

San Fernando, Vessigny and Point Fortin area:

Erline's, 143 Pond Street,
La Romain ☎ 657-3749

South Beach Villa, Vessigny Village,
La Brea ☎ 648-9328

Vanessa's Cottage,
71 Clifton Hill, Point Fortin
☎ 648-2468

Tobago

Annabel's, Glendales Drive,
Mt. Irvine ☎ 639-8357

Ann's Villa, Bacolet Street,
Scarborough ☎ 639-5200

Auntie Pearl's, Government House
Road, Scarborough ☎ 639-2901

Belleviste Apartments,
Sandy Point ☎ 639-9351

Cedra Lewis Baird,
Charlotteville ☎ 660-5125

Cholson Chalets, Man O' War Bay,
Charlotteville ☎ 639-8553

Coral Ridge Studio Apartment,
Crown Point ☎ 639-0118

Crystal View,
Scarborough ☎ 639-2075

Federal Villa, Crooks River,
Scarborough ☎ 639-3926

Golf View Apartments, Old Grange,
Mount Irvine ☎ 639-9551

Hill Crest, Orlanda Drive,
Bethany ☎ 639-9263

Marie's, Lot 40, Mt. Irvine Development, Mt. Irvine ☎ 639-8176

Moore's Guesthouse, Belle Air,
Charlotteville ☎ 660-4749

Plantation House, Ist Street,
Bacolet Gardens ☎ 639-2327

Point's Inn, Buccoo ☎ 639-7064

Quality Inn, Carnbee ☎ 639-7571

R & G's Holiday Home,
Carnbee ☎ 639-7571

Sand Castle, Mt. Irvine ☎ 639-2353

Sandy's, Fort and Robinson Streets,
Scarborough ☎ 639-2737

Sea Edge, Mt. Irvine ☎ 639-9052

Stella B Apartments, 79 Bacolet
Street, Scarborough ☎ 639-5603

Tony's House, Carnbee ☎ 639-8836

Uptown Inn, Cuyler and Main Street,
Scarborough ☎ 639-2589

Viola's Place, Lowlands, ☎ 639-9441

Windy Hill, Bethel ☎ 639-8836

Woods Castle Holiday Resorts,
Batteaux Bay, Speyside, ☎ 639-0803

Tobago Villas Agency PO Box 301,
Scarborough ☎ 639-8737

Cricket is the national game and played with such enthusiasm that it is not surprising that the West Indies are world champions. Trinidad has produced many cricketing greats, including Brian Lara 'The Prince of Port of Spain', who has broken many of the sport's batting records. Easter normally marks the start of the season with visiting Test teams, but the game is played at every opportunity and anywhere. You can be driving in the countryside, turn a corner and confront 'Trini' players using the road as a wicket. It is played on the beach and even in the water if the tide is coming in. If an island team or the West Indies is playing, almost all the radios on the islands are tuned in for the commentary. Even if you are not that interested in the game, it is worth going along to The Oval if there is a match on just to enjoy the Carnival-like atmosphere with steel bands and very boisterous but good-natured spectators. And, when cricket is not being played, football is the top sport with basketball also becoming very popular. The two main sporting venues are The Oval, one of the best cricket test match grounds in the world, and the National Stadium that is used for football and athletics. The Jean Pierre Complex next door to the stadium is a venue for a wide range of indoor and outdoor sports, including basketball, boxing, hockey, netball, tennis and volleyball.

For the visitor, there is a huge range of sporting opportunities from swimming and scuba diving, to horseback riding and hiking, to golf and tennis. One of the best-rated golf courses is the championship 18-hole St. Andrew's Club at Moka, north of Port of Spain. You can also play at the public course at Chauaramas, and at Pointe-a-Pierre, where the 18th hole runs alongside the nature center. There are also 9-hole courses at Seville and Brighton.

The Country Club in Maraval hosts junior and senior tennis tournaments and offers all the latest facilities for visitors. There is cycling, kayaking with a new kayaking facility in Chaguaramas, sailing, squash and, of course, fishing either from shore or boat. The Atlantic coastline offers stronger swell for windsurfing and surfing but the seas can sometimes be very rough and care is needed, while the Caribbean beaches offer safe swimming.

There are lots of spectator sports as well, such as horse racing at Santa Rosa (☎ 646-2450), The grueling du Maurier Great Race power boat run from Trinidad to Tobago every July, the Carib International Game Fishing Tournament in April, and the Angostura/Yachting World Regatta in May (Did you know that Angostura Bitters come from Trinidad?). There are even goat and crab races on Tobago!

Most hotels offer a variety of sports and water activities, and there are diving schools where you can learn what it is all about and progress to advanced level if you have the time.

Walking is great fun and there are lots of trails, especially in the mountains but have stout, non-slip footwear and a waterproof. Protect yourself against insects, carry adequate drinking water and keep an eye on the time, because night falls quickly and you don't want to be caught out on the trail after dark. Guides can be arranged to escort you on these walks and make sure you get the most out of your trip.

FISHING

Fishing is a favourite pursuit, and many islanders will fish for hours from quayside walls, from the beach or riverside. Deep sea and game fishing is mostly for dolphin (the fish 'dorado' not the mammal), blue marlin and tuna which can weight up to 1,000lbs, wahoo and white marlin, which can weigh more than 100lbs, tarpon and the fighting sailfish. The four-day Carib International Game Fishing Tournament takes place on Tobago every year, usually at the end of April or early in May.

Snapper, grouper, bonito, dorado and barracuda can all be caught close to shore. There are a number of boats available for charter or which offer deep-sea fishing. Operators include:

Trinidad

Classic Sportfishing Charters ☎ 637-3897

Dream Weaver ☎ 634-2213

Executive Charters ☎ 627-6345

Island Yacht Charters, Victoria Gardens, Diego Martin ☎ 637-7389

South Caribbean Charterers, Chaguaramas ☎ 637-3636

Trinidad and Tobago Game Fishing Association, Cascade Road, Cascade ☎ 624-5304

Tobago

Hard Play Fishing Cruises ☎ 639-7108

FITNESS GYMS

Many of the resort hotels have fitness suites, gyms and spas. Other facilities include:

Body Works, West Mall, West Moorings ☎ 637-4545

Fitness Centre, Diego Martin Shopping Center ☎ 637-7765

Forever Fit, 18 Elizabeth Street, St. Clair ☎ 622-4014

Jumbo Gym, Curepe ☎ 622-4014

La Joya Sporting Complex, Eastern Main Road, St. Joseph ☎ 662-1192

Peter Fung's Fitness Gym, Normandie Hotel ☎ 624-1181

Universal Fitness, 11 Eastern Main Road, Tunapuna ☎ 645-0047

GOLF

Trinidad

Brighton Golf Course, La Brea, 9 holes.

Chaguaramas Public Golf Course, 9 holes ☎ 634-4349.

St. Andrew's Golf Club, Moka, Maraval, 18-holes ☎ 629-2314.

Tobago

Mount Irvine Golf Club, Mount Irvine Bay Hotel ☎ 639-8871

Tobago Plantations Lowlands Estate Golf and Country Club ☎ 639-8000

HORSEBACK RIDING

Palm Tree Village Beach Resort, Lambeau, Tobago ☎ 639-4347

SQUASH

The following are private clubs but non-members can usually get a game by making an early booking.

Trinidad

Pelican Squash Club, Pelican Inn, Cascade ☎ 637-4888

Valley Vue Hotel, Ariapita Road, St. Ann's ☎ 623-3511

Tobago

Grafton Beach Resort, Black Rock ☎ 639-0191

TENNIS

Almost all the resorts and many of the hotels have their own tennis courts, often floodlit. If newly arrived on the island, book a court early in the morning or late in the afternoon when it is cooler until you acclimatize to the heat. In addition you can play in **Trinidad** at:

Arima Tennis Club, Railway Road, Arima ☎ 667-3526

Trinidad Country Club, Long Circular Road, Maraval ☎ 622-3470

Princes Building Grounds, Upper Frederick Street, Port of Spain ☎ 623-1121

Skinner Park, San Fernando ☎ 657-7168

Tranquility Square Lawn Tennis Club, Victoria Avenue, Port of Spain ☎ 625-4182.

On **Tobago** there are courts at:

Blue Waters Inn, Speyside ☎ 660-2583

Le Gran Courlan ☎ 639-9667 Mount Irvine Bay Hotel, Mount Irvine ☎ 639-8871.

SCUBA

Most of the diving is off Tobago and its smaller offshore islands, and there are scores of excellent dive sites to explore and enjoy. The marine life off Tobago is so diverse and prolific that one world traveled scuba diver insists it is the equal of Australia's Great Barrier Reef. The clear, warm waters certainly offer world-class diving with underwater visibility often more than 100ft (30m), but more generally between 60 and 80ft (18 and 24m). Average water temperature is around 75°F (24°C).

One of the star attractions of diving off Tobago is being able to swim with the giant manta rays, some of them 12ft (3.6m) from wing tip to wing tip, and another is that many offshore areas are still largely unexplored. The best place to swim with, and even stroke the manta rays, is off Little Tobago, where about a dozen glide through the waters.

The hills of Tobago fall steeply into the sea to form cliffs, sheer walls and canyons, with underwater tunnels, trenches and caves to explore. The range of hard and soft corals is staggering. Every known species of hard coral and most of the soft corals can be found, including the world's largest known brain coral – 12ft (3.6m) high and 16ft (4.8m) across.

The waters are so rich in marine life because the Guyana Current, fed by the Orinoco River, moves up the north eastern coast of South America, divides around Trinidad and washes the south and east coasts of Tobago. The warm, nutrient rich waters attract large numbers of deep-sea fish that can be seen much closer to the surface than normal. It is not unusual to spot barracuda, dolphin, whale sharks and turtles, as well as teeming shoals of smaller fish such as butterfly fish, queen and French angels, damsels, parrotfish, grunts, and rarer species such as tarpon and trigger fish.

There is a wide selection of dive sites from easy ones suitable for novices to hard ones for the most experienced. The easiest dive sites and the safest for novice divers are on the shallow reefs off the west coast, like Buccoo Reef, and the sheltered dives around Goat and Little Tobago Islands. Most of the other sites are better suited for experienced divers able to cope with quite strong currents and, at the northern end of the island, with moderate to high seas.

The best dive areas are on the south and west coasts between Pigeon Point and Castara, and on the north east coast from Speyside to Charlotteville, including the rocky offshore islands of Little Tobago and St Giles.

Along the calmer, western coast there are long sandy beaches with a gentle offshore slope to the extensive fringing reefs of hard and soft corals, and then dropping away with rocky cliffs.

The east coast has deeper water with larger and more rocky fringing reefs, with plunging underwater cliffs and rock formations, submarine mountains and plenty of large ocean fish, especially around the offshore islands.

Diving is usually from pirogues, the traditional island fishing boat with high pointed bow, which is ideal for local conditions. It does mean, however, that you normally board by wading in from the beach.

The main dive facilities and dive sites on Tobago are:

Charlotteville – from where it is a short trip across to St Giles island where there are natural rock formations such as London Bridge, Booby Reef, The Sisters, Marble Island and Fishbowl. London Bridge Rock, is a natural rock arch carved out by the sea while below water; it is a mass of crevices and swim-through holes.

The Sisters is a group of steep-sided pinnacles which descend to 130ft (40m), and which are home to large numbers of large fish.

The area off Charlotteville is referred to locally as **Northside**, and it is noted for its underwater cliffs and canyons. The waters can be rough and there are strong currents that restrict it to experienced divers only. Conditions can prevent diving, but when it is possible, it is a memorable experience.

Speyside – this small fishing village on Tyrrel's Bay on the north-east end of the island, is the best departure point for the two offshore islets of Goat Island and Little Tobago, and if you want to meet the manta rays. Both islands lie about a mile (1.6km) offshore and their sheltered coves and inlets offer safe and spectacular diving. Flying Manta is an area of massive boulders and brain coral lying between the two islets, and is a favourite feeding ground of Atlantic mantas.

There are many other dive sites to choose from, such as Batteaux Reef, **Angel Reef, Kelliston Drain, Lau's reef, The Cathedral, John Rock, Bookends** noted for tarpon and so called because two large rocks break the surface. **Japanese Gardens** is one of the most beautiful reefs lying in 40 to 85ft (12 to 26m) of water, and

is noted for its mass of waving soft corals and sponges. **Blackjack Hole** is a large reef site frequented by the fish that give it its name. These streamlined predators are rare in many parts of the Caribbean but thrive in these waters. Large mantas can also often be seen at this site.

Batteaux Bay offers exciting diving because of contesting currents, as does **Kamikaze Cut**, where expert divers can ride a fierce current between two vertical rock faces.

Crown Point – on the south-west tip of the island, is a good base for exploring **The Shallows** – a submarine plateau lying between 50 and 100ft (15 and 30m) and a popular haunt of turtles, dolphins, angelfish, nurse sharks and sometimes, larger ones like tiger sharks. It is about three miles (5km) off the south-west of the island in the channel between Tobago and Trinidad. Because of the strong currents, the drift dives have to be carefully managed. You can also visit the fast drift **Flying Reef** where you can see rays and morays.

West Coast – the coastline has beach-lined bays fringed with reefs that extend from nearly all the rocky points that lie between them.

Buccoo Reef is said to get its name from the French word 'beaucoup', and is at an average depth of 40ft (12m) and offers safe diving in calmer waters.

One of the most popular dive sites is the **Mount Irvine Wall** in about 60ft (16m) with masses of crevices and ledges, where you might see eagle rays during the day, and octopus, moray eel, lobster, short nosed batfish and orange ball anemones during night dives. There is also **The Sisters**, another wall that descends to 140ft (43m).

Arnos Vale Reef is at a depth of 40ft (12m), and is really a series of reefs parallel to the shore, with moray eels, stingrays and sometimes, the torpedo ray. Off the South West Coast there are the **Bopez, Kethcup and Kariwak** to explore.

DIVE OPERATORS

Tobago

Adventure Eco-Divers, Grafton Beach Resort, ☎ 639-8729

Aquamarine Dive, Blue Waters Inn, Speyside ☎660-5445

Manta Dice Centre, Pigeon Point, ☎ 639-9209

Man Friday Diving, Charlotteville ☎ 660-4676

Mt Irvine Bay Watersports ☎ 639-4721

Proscuba Dive, Bon Accord ☎ 639-7424

R and Sea Divers Den, Crown Point ☎ 639-8120

Ron's Watersports, Main Road, Charlotteville ☎ 622-0459

Scuba Adventure safaris, Pigeon Point ☎660-7333

Tobago Dive Experience, Turtle Beach Hotel ☎ 639-7034, and Manta Lodge, Speyside ☎ 660-4888

Tobago Divemasters, Speyside ☎ 660-5924

Undersea Tobago, Mt. Irvine Hotel ☎ 639-7759

Wild Turtle Dive, Pigeon Point ☎ 639-7936

World of Watersport, Tobago Hilton ☎ 660-7234

Trinidad

Ron's Watersports, Western Main Road, Cocorite ☎ 622-0459

Scuba Specialists, Kajim Street, Marabella ☎ 658-3861

WATER SPORTS

Trinidad

Surfing and windsurfing are the main watersports activities. Specialist operators include:

Ron's Watersports, Western Main Road, Cocorite ☎ 673-0549

Surfing Association of Trinidad and Tobago ☎ 623-0920

Windsurfing Association of Trinidad and Tobago ☎ 659-2457

Tobago

Blue Waters Inn ☎ 660-2583

Dillons Deep Sea Charters ☎ 639-8765

Grafton Beach Resort ☎ 639-0191

Kalina Cats ☎ 639-6306

Loafer Cruises ☎ 639-7312

Le Gran Courland ☎ 639-9667

Mt. Irvine Watersports ☎ 639-9379

GETTING THERE

By air – Piarco International Airport on Trinidad and Crown Point Airport on Tobago have inter-island connections and links with North and South America, Western Europe and the Caribbean.

Major North American gateways connecting with Trinidad are Miami and New York in the US, and Toronto in Canada. San Juan, on Puerto Rico is the main Caribbean gateway, while European major gateways are London in the UK, Frankfurt in Germany and Zurich in Switzerland. There are also connections via Caracas in Venezuela. It is 3.5 hours flying time from Miami, 4.5 hours from New York and 8 hours from London.

Getting to Trinidad

From Europe – British Airways and BWIA (British West Indian Airways – and known locally as BeeWee) that is the national airline of Trinidad and Tobago, fly from London and Lufthansa flies direct from Frankfurt and Zurich. There are also charter flights from Amsterdam, Cologne, Munich and Stockholm. Highest fares are in December and during the summer.

From North America – BWIA flies nonstop from both islands to Miami and New York. It also flies between Trinidad and Toronto.

Air Canada has services from Toronto with connection flights to other Canadian cities, and American Airlines flies from Miami with connections to other US cities.

Air Caribbean offers linking flights between Trinidad and Tobago. BWIA also flies to San Juan in Puerto Rico, and Kingston Jamaica, and also operates between Antigua, Barbados, St. Lucia, St. Kitts and Grenada. BWIA's new Tobago Express offers services between Trinidad and Tobago.

From other Caribbean islands – LIAT flies between Trinidad and Anguilla, Antigua, Barbados, Barbuda, Grenada, Guadeloupe, Guyana, Montserrat, Nevis, Puerto Rico, St. Thomas and St. Kitts.

Getting to Tobago

There are BWIA flights from Miami and New York, many inter-island flights daily as well as flights to a number of other Caribbean islands. Britannia flies from London and Condor, the Lufthansa subsidiary flies from Frankfurt. Air Express flies between Trinidad and Tobago.

Note: LIAT has a number of special passes, which are some of the best air deals anywhere and allow you to island-hop at bargain basement prices. There are the Explorer and Super Explorer Fares, which allow you to fly to several Caribbean islands on one trip at a flat fare, while the LIAT Airpass allows visitors from Europe to fly to between three and six islands at a rate of $360 off-peak and $210 peak per island. The Airpass is valid for 21 days from the start of the first LIAT flight, and must be bought in Europe together with an inter-national ticket to the Caribbean.

Note: Hot weather in the Caribbean can often lead to turbulence, and if you are island hopping in small aircraft, you may experience a bumpier ride than you are used to in larger planes. Do not worry, the turbulence rarely lasts long, and the views from the air more than make up for it.

By sea – Port of Spain is the main commercial port while Point Fortin, Point a Pierre and Brighton in the south, handle petroleum exports. Cruise ships also visit Port of Spain and Scarborough. If you want to travel the islands, the best thing to do is to visit a marina and see if any of the boats want crew or are willing to take a passenger. There is a ferry between Trinidad and Tobago which sails daily except Saturday. Monday to Friday it sails from Port of Spain at 2pm and leaves Scarborough at 11am. On Sunday it departs Port of Spain at 11am and Scarborough at 11pm. The crossing takes 5.5 hours. Windward Lines operate steamships between Trinidad, St Vincent, Barbados and Venezuela. It sails from Port of Spain at 4pm each Thursday calling at St Vincent and Barbados and returning to Trinidad on Tuesday. And, on Tuesday it sails from Trinidad at 5pm for Venezuela, arriving at 9.30pm.

ARRIVAL, ENTRY REQUIREMENTS AND CUSTOMS

An immigration form has to be filled in and presented on arrival. The form requires you to say where you will be staying on the island, and if you plan to move around, put down the first hotel you will be staying at. The immigration form is in two parts, one of which is stamped and returned to you in your passport. You must retain this until departure when the slip is retrieved as you check in at the airport.

North American, British citizens and those from European Community and most Commonwealth countries need a valid passport for entry, but a visa is not required. The exceptions include citizens from Australia, Cuba, Mexico, New Zealand, Nigeria, Papua New Guinea, Sri Lanka, Tanzania and Uganda. Visitors from other countries should check with their travel agent before begining your trip. You may be asked to show that you have a return ticket before being admitted.

If visiting on business, a confirming letter may prove helpful in speeding your way through customs, especially if traveling with samples.

Having cleared immigration, you will have to go through customs, and it is quite usual to have to open your luggage for inspection. If you have expensive cameras, jewels, etc. it is a good idea to travel with a photocopy of the receipt.

Visitors entering Trinidad and Tobago are allowed to bring in duty free one quart of liquor, 200 cigarettes or 50 cigars and gifts up to the value of TT$1200.

Visa

All visitors need a valid passport. Visitors who are not citizens of the US, UK, Commonwealth and European Community countries, may require visas.

Inoculations

Inoculations are only required for visitors traveling from infected areas.

AIRLINES

Air Canada	☎ 669-4065
Air Caribbean	☎ 623-2500
Air Jamaica	☎ 624-5688ALM ☎ 623-8243
American Airlines	☎ 669-4661
British Airways	☎ 639-0588
BWIA	☎ 1-800-538-2942 or 627-2942, Tobago 639-8741
LIAT	☎ 627-6274
Surinam Airways	☎ 627-4747
United Airways	☎ 623-8201

Banks

Banks are open from 8am to 2pm Monday to Friday and from 8am to 12 noon and additionally from 3pm to 5pm on Friday.

Banks include:

Citibank, 12 Queen's Park East, Port of Spain ☎ 625-1046

First Citizens Bank, 50 St Vincent Street, Port of Spain ☎ 623-2576

Republic Bank has 32 branches throughout the islands and 42 ATM machines, Independence Square, Port of Spain ☎ 625-4412.

Royal Bank of Trinidad and Tobago, Independence Square, Port of Spain ☎ 625-3511

Western Union, has 21 locations in Trinidad and Tobago (for money transfer) ☎ 623-6000

BEACHES

The islands have fabulous beaches, everything you ever dreamed of for a tropical island, golden sand, a fringe of tall palms for shade, and turquoise clear warm seas. Generally the best beaches are along the north and east coasts. On the north coast Maracas Bay and Las Cuevas are the most popular beaches but there are many others, like Blanchisseuse, and some are difficult to reach without hiking, but their beauty and solitude make the trip worthwhile. There are lovely beaches along the east coast between Matura Bay in the north and Mayaro to the south. On the south coast there are good beaches at Guayaguayare, Moruga and west of Roja Point such as Palo Seco, and on the southwest peninsula at Guapo Bay south of La Brea.

BEAUTY SALONS AND HAIRDRESSERS

Many of the resorts have their own facilities.

BICYCLE RENTALS

Tobago

Island Bikes, Milford Road, Bon Accord   ☎ 639-8587

Mapp's Multi Service, Milford Road   ☎ 639-7464

CAMPING

Camping is allowed in designated areas and on some beaches that can only be reached by hiking, but there are no facilities so you have to carry in all your supplies and water.

CAR RENTAL

Cars and four-wheel drive vehicles can be hired and provide the best way of exploring the island. If you plan to go at peak periods, it is best to hire your vehicle in advance through your travel agent. Cars can be hired, however, at airports, hotels or car hire offices on the island. A valid international driving permit is required, or a valid US, Canadian, French, German, Bahamian or UK licence can be used for 90 days.

Hire car rates range from TT$180 a day for a small vehicle up to TT$450 for a large car, with reductions for longer rentals. Prices do vary, however, from company to company and it pays to shop around if you have not booked in advance. Prices are more competitive on Tobago, and four-wheel drive vehicles can be hired from around TT$156 although larger off the road vehicles cost more. Motorbikes can be rented from about TT$120-150 a day.

Before accepting the vehicle, check it for scratches, dents and other problems, such as missing wing mirrors, and make sure these are clearly listed. Also check there is a spare wheel in good condition and a working jack. While there are several service stations around the island it is a good idea always to keep your fuel tank topped up.

Rules of the road

Drive on the LEFT. The roads are generally good and there is a substantial road improvement schedule under way. In rural areas, however, you have to be on the look out for potholes, fallen branches, coconuts in the roads and so on. Do not speed because you never know what may be round the next corner. The islanders' love of cricket encourages them to play at every opportunity, and the road makes an ideal wicket!

Drinking and driving is against the law, and there are heavy penalties if convicted, especially if it resulted in an accident.

Avoid clearly marked 'no parking' zones or you might pick up a ticket, but parking generally does not pose a problem.

If you have an accident or breakdown during the day, call your car hire company, so make sure you have the telephone number with you. They will usually send out a mechanic or a replacement vehicle.

Fact File

If you are stuck at night make sure the car is off the road, lock the vehicle and call a taxi to take you back to your hotel. Report the problem to the car hire company or the police as soon as possible.

Hire companies are:

Trinidad

Port of Spain:

Auto Rentals ☎ 675-7638

Autocenter ☎ 628-8800

Carnetta's Inn ☎ 622-5165

Convenient Rental ☎ 634-4017

Discount ☎ 622-6596

Econo Cars Rental ☎ 622-8072

Monique's ☎ 628-3334

Singh's Auto Rentals ☎ 623-0150

Piarco International Airport:

Auto Rentals ☎ 669-2277

Econo ☎ 669-2342

Reesal's ☎ 669-3330

Singh's Auto Rentals ☎ 669-5417

Sue's ☎ 669-1635

Thrifty ☎ 669-0602

San Fernando:

Auto Rentals ☎ 657-7368

Singh's ☎ 636-7959

Tobago

Amar Rentals,
Milford Road ☎ 639-7491

Auto Rentals,
Crown Point Airport ☎ 639-0644

Baird's Rental (cars, motorcycles and scooters), Scarborough ☎ 639-2528

Econo Cars ☎ 660-8728

Hill Crest Car Rental, ☎ 639-5208

Peter Gremli Car Rental, Mt. Pelier Terrace, Crown Point ☎ 639-8400

Rattan's RL Car Rental, Crown Point ☎ 639-8271

Rodriguez Travel (Thrifty),
Bethany ☎ 639-8507

Sherman's ☎ 639-2292

Singh's Auto Rentals, Grafton Beach Resort, Black Rock ☎ 639-0624

Ted's Sunshine Enterprises ☎ 639-0547

Thrifty ☎ 639-8111/8507

Waukie's ☎ 639-9072

CURRENCY

The official currency on the island is the Trinidad and Tobago dollar (TT$). It is the only legal currency on the island and it floats against other currencies. There are 1, 5, 10, 20 and 100 TT$ notes and 1, 5, 10, 25, and 50 TT cent coins. Daily rates are carried in the newspapers, and listed in banks and at hotel exchange desks. Always keep receipts of all money transactions so that unspent TT$ can be exchanged back at the end of your trip.

Credit cards are widely accepted in tourist areas and by most car hire companies, hotels, restaurants and large stores. There are also ATM machines available in Port of Spain. The American Express representative on Trinidad is The Travel Centre, Uptown Mall, Level 2, Edward Street, Port of Spain ☎ 625-1636.

Note: Always have a few small denomination notes for tips.

DEPARTURE TAX

There is a departure tax of TT$85 plus TT$15 security tax for all passengers leaving the island. The tax must be paid in local currency.

DISABLED PERSONS – FACILITIES

There are some facilities for the disabled at most of the larger resorts, but not much elsewhere.

DRESS CODE

Casual and lightweight is the key but you can be as smart or as cool as you like. Beachwear is fine for the beach and pool areas, but cover up a little for the street. Wear a hat if planning to be out in the sun for a long time. Dressing up for dinner can be fun, but I do not know of anywhere where ties have to be worn.

ELECTRICITY

The usual electricity supply is 110 or 220 volts AC, 60 cycles that is suitable for most US appliances. Adaptors are generally available at the hotels, or can be purchased if you do not travel with your own.

EMBASSIES AND CONSULATES

Canada, Maple House, Sweet Briar Road, St. Clair ☎ 622-6232

Italy, CDC Complex, Eastern Main Road, Champs Fleurs ☎ 622-0391

France, 6th Floor, 11 Maraval Road, Port of Spain ☎ 622-7446

Japan, 5 Hayes Street, St. Clair ☎ 628-5991

Germany, 7-9 Marli Street, Newtown ☎ 628-1630

UK, 19 St. Clair Avenue, St. Clair ☎ 628-1234/2748

Holland, 3rd floor, 69-71 Edward Street, Port of Spain ☎ 625-1210

US, 15 Queen's Park West, Port of Spain ☎ 622-6371

EMERGENCY TELEPHONE NUMBERS

For police dial 999 or 622-5412,
For fire and ambulance dial 990.

ESSENTIAL THINGS TO PACK

Sun tan cream, sunglasses, sun hat, camera (and lots of film), insect repellant, and binoculars if interested in bird watching and wildlife, and a small torch in case of power failures.

Fact File

FESTIVALS/CALENDAR OF EVENTS

January	1 January New Year's Day
February	Pan Around The Neck Panorama, Independence Square, Port of Spain Carnival
March	Good Friday, Easter Sunday and Monday (dates vary)
April	Hindu Festival of Phagwa (Hindu New Year) Goat and crab racing. Buccoo, Tobago Carib International Game Fishing Tournament, Tobago
May	Pan Ramajay Angostura Yachting World Regatta 30 May Arrival Day
June	19 June Labor Day Muslim Festival of Hosay (date varies)
July	Tobago Heritage Festival
August	1 August Emancipation Day 31 August Independence Day Santa Rosa Festival, Arima
September	24 September Republic Day Carnival King and Queen of the World Competition
October	Hindu Festival of Divali The World Steel Band Music Festival and the School Steel Band Festival are held on alternate years. Annual Orchid Show
November	Pan Jazz Festival
December	Parang, Trinidad's own seasonal music, played on four stringed cuatros and sung in pigeon Spanish. 25 December – Christmas Day 26 December – Boxing Day 31 December – Old Year's Night

GAMBLING

There are no casinos on Trinidad or Tobago

GALLERIES

Apart from the National Art Gallery there are a number of excellent private galleries in Port of Spain. These include:

Art Creators Gallery, 7 St. Ann's Road, St. Ann's ☎ 624-4369

Caribbean Contemporary Arts Centre, Building 7, Fernandes Estate ☎ 625-1889

Gallery 1,2,3,4, The Normandie,
10 Nook Avenue, St. Ann's
☎ 625-5502

101 Gallery, 101 Tragarete Road,
Woodbrook ☎ 628-4081

On Location, Upper Level,
West Mall ☎ 633-3404

Upper Room Art Gallery,
Mount St. Benedict ☎ 645-1905

HEALTH

There are no serious health problems although visitors should take
precautions against the sun and mosquitoes, both of which can ruin
your holiday. Immunization is not required unless traveling from an
infected area within six days of arrival.

All hotels have doctors either resident or on call.

Tanning safely

The sun is very strong but sea breezes often disguise just how hot it
is. If you are not used to the sun, take it carefully for the first two or
three days, use a good sunscreen with a factor of 15 or higher, and
do not sunbathe during the hottest parts of the day. Wear sunglasses
and a sun hat. Sunglasses will protect you against the glare, especially strong on the beach, and sun hats will protect your head.

If you spend a lot of time swimming or scuba diving, take extra
care, as you will burn even more quickly because of the combination
of salt water and sun. Calamine lotion and preparations containing
aloe are both useful in combating sunburn.

Irritating insects

Mosquitoes can be a problem almost anywhere. In your room, burn
mosquito coils or use one of the many electrical devices that burn an
insect repelling tablet. Mosquitoes are not so much of a problem on
or near the beaches because of onshore winds, but they may well
bite you as you enjoy an open-air evening meal. Use a good insect
repellant, especially if planning a trip into the rain forests.

Lemon grass can be found growing naturally, and a handful of this
in your room is also a useful mosquito deterrent.

Sand flies can be a problem on the beach. Despite their tiny size
they can give you a nasty bite. And, ants abound, so make sure you
check the ground carefully before sitting down otherwise you might
get bitten, and the bites can itch for days.

Note: Drinking water from the tap is safe although bottled mineral
and distilled water are widely available.

HOSPITALS

There are hospitals in Port of Spain, Scarborough, Mount Hope and
San Fernando, as well as many clinics and health centers around the
islands. The main ones are:

General Hospital,
Charlotte Street, Port of Spain
☎ 623-2951

Eric Williams Medical Sciences
Complex, Mount Hope
☎ 645-HOPE

View over the Port of Spain, Trinidad

Fact File

Community Hospital, Western
Main Road, Cocorite ☎ 622-1191

Scarborough Hospital,
☎ 639-2551.

St. Clair Medical Centre, Elizabeth
Street, St. Clair, Port of Spain
☎ 628-1451

LANGUAGE

The official language spoken is English, although it includes many words that have been imported from other European and African languages, so it can sound a little strange and does take some getting used to. The old French-based Patois has almost died out, although Hindi is still spoken among the Indian community, especially in the central region.

There are a few very descriptive words that are worth knowing. A *jump up* is a dance or impromptu party, and gets its name because the music is so foot tapping you have to jump up and join in. A *fete* is another word for a party, and it is a good place to *free up,* which means to relax and just enjoy yourself without worrying about what others might think. And, if the party is really going well and everyone is having a good time, it is a *bacchanal*. And, do not get confused by words like lime and wine. To *lime* is to watch the girls go by, while a *wine* is a very sexy dance.

LOST PROPERTY

Report lost property as soon as possible to your hotel or the nearest police station.

MEDIA

There are 3 daily newspapers (the Express, Guardian and NewsDay), one tri-weekly, several weeklies, many radio stations as well as Government and commercial TV stations plus US cable channels. Major international newspapers and magazines are also available.

MUSIC

Music is a way of life and the philosophy is the louder it is played, the better, and once the music starts it goes on for hours. Parties often last all night.

NIGHTLIFE

There is no shortage of nightlife and you can find clubs, pubs and bars where you can listen to lively music into the small hours. There are discos for dancing and most resort hotels offer their own live entertainment. Fetes, large public jump ups are often held, especially in the weeks before and during Carnival. Nightspots include:

The Anchorage, Point Gourde Road, Chaguaramas ☎ 634-4334

Baba's On The Bay, Western Main Road, Carenage ☎ 637-2222

Bamboo Room, Tropical Hotel, Rookery Nook, Maraval ☎ 622-5815

Carnival Bar, Trinidad Hilton, Port of Spain ☎ 624-3211

Cascade Club, The Normandie, St. Ann's ☎ 624-1181

Chaconia Inn, 106 Saddle Road, Maraval ☎ 628-8603

Gazebo, Trinidad Hilton, Port of Spain ☎ 624-3211

Lobby Bar, Trinidad Hilton, Port of Spain ☎ 624-3211

Maple Lounge Bar, Holiday Inn, Wrightson Road, Port of Spain ☎ 625-3361

Pelican Inn Pub, Coblentz Avenue, Cascade ☎ 624-7486

Rafters, 6 Warner Street, Newtown ☎ 628-9258

Royal Palm Suite Hotel, Saddle Road, Maraval ☎ 628-5086

Villa Maria, 48a Perseverence Road, Haleland Park, Maraval ☎ 629-8023

Wazo Deyzeel, Carib Way, St. Ann's ☎ 623-0115

PERSONAL INSURANCE AND MEDICAL COVER

Make sure you have adequate personal insurance and medical cover. If you need to call out a doctor or have medical treatment, you will probably have to pay for it at the time, so keep all receipts so that you can reclaim on your insurance.

PHARMACIES

There are a number of pharmacies and many of these stay open late in the evening, including:

Alchemists, 57 Duke Street, Port of Spain ☎ 623-2718

Hilton Pharmacy, Hilton Hotel, Port of Spain ☎ 624-3211

Kappa Drugs, St. James ☎ 622-5645

Medicine Plus. Ellerslie Plaza, Maraval ☎ 622-8768

Royal Palm Pharmacy, Royal Palm Plaza, Maraval ☎ 628-3660

and several along Western Main Road.

In San Fernando there is Tiaren, Coffee Street ☎652-3368

On Tobago there is Scarborough Drugs, Carrington Street and Wilson Road ☎ 639-4161

PHOTOGRAPHY

The intensity of the sun can play havoc with your films, especially if photographing near water or white sand. Compensate for the brightness otherwise your photographs will come out over exposed and wishy-washy. The heat can actually damage film so store reels in a box or bag in the hotel fridge if there is one. Also remember to protect your camera if on the beach, as a single grain of sand is all it takes to jam the mechanism.

It is very easy to get 'click happy' in the Caribbean, but be tactful when taking photographs. Many islanders are shy or simply fed up with being photographed, and others will insist on a small payment. You will have to decide whether the picture is worth it, but if a person declines to have their photograph taken, don't ignore this.

POLICE

Central Police Station, Port of Spain ☎ 625-4067
Scarborough Police Station ☎ 639-2512

POST OFFICES

The main post offices are: Golden Grove, Piarco, Trinidad; and Wilson Road, Scarborough in Tobago.

PUBLIC TOILETS

There are not many public toilets on the island, but bars, restaurants and hotels have private facilities that can usually be used if you ask politely.

RESTAURANTS

There is a remarkably large choice when it comes to eating out on the islands. There are the inevitable fast food burger, pizza and fried chicken outlets, beach cafés offering excellent value for money and elegant upscale dining rooms, as well as restaurants offering a wide range of ethnic cuisines, from Creole and Caribbean cooking to Latin American and Chinese.

Most accept credit cards and during peak times of the year, reservations are recommended. If you come across a restaurant not listed in the guide, or have comments about any of those that are, I would very much like to hear from you.

The restaurants listed in the itineraries are classified by price ($ inexpensive, $$ moderate, $$$ expensive),   based on quality of food, service and ambience.

SECURITY

It makes sense like anywhere else, not to walk around wearing expensive jewels or flashing large sums of money.

Do not carry around your passport, traveler checks/travellers cheques or all your money. Keep them secure in your room or in a hotel safety deposit box. It is also a good idea to have photocopies of the information page of your passport, your air ticket and holiday insurance policy. All will help greatly if the originals are lost.

As with most tourist destinations, you might be pestered by touts trying to sell tours, souvenirs and even drugs, or by young people begging. A firm 'no' or 'not interested', is normally enough to persuade them to try someone else. It is safer to take a taxi late at night and do not stray into lonely, dark or unfamiliar areas, and if driving, be very wary if someone tries to flag you down.

SERVICE CHARGES AND TAXES

There is VAT of 15% on most goods, and a Government tax of 10% on all hotel rooms plus a service charge of 10% or higher is added. Menus and tariffs sometimes include these charges so check to make sure they have not been added again. In shops, the price on the label is what you pay. When buying in markets and from street vendors, try haggling over the price.

SHOPPING

There is a wide range of shops, from up market malls with the latest high fashions, to craft shops and wayside vendors. Best buys include local leather work, pottery, paintings by local artists, hand made jewels, hand designed fabrics, steel band pans and soca CDs, as well as the fiery pepper sauce.

Shops are usually open between 8am and 4pm Monday to Friday, and 8am to noon on Saturday, although malls tend to open and close later, usually 10am to 7pm Monday to Saturday.

There are scores of shops to explore in downtown Port of Spain starting with the upscale stores and galleries in the Cruise Ship Complex. There are large malls in the suburbs in St. James and Westmoorings. There are boutiques in Maraval, and an upscale mini mall known as The Market at the Hotel Normandie. Charlotte Street is great for its sidewalk stalls. Grand Bazzaar, West Mall and Long Circular Mall offer a wide range of imported goods while Ellerslie Court has boutiques and shops offering batik, pottery and other arts and crafts. Also worth visiting is the Kapok Shopping Arcade.

San Fernando offers more traditional shopping at Gulf City, a sprawling covered bazaar, and you can buy traditional Indian goods, clothes, spices, pottery, brassware and music in Chaguanas and the nearby village of Edinburgh, in the area known as Little India.

SIGHTSEEING

Sightseeing and island tours by land or sea can be arranged through hotels, tour representatives or one of the many specialist tour companies on the islands. All offer a number of trips and excursions, or can tailor itineraries to suit you. Many of the tours sound the same, so check to see that you are getting value for money, or getting something special.

These include:

Trinidad

A's Travel Service, 177 Tragarete Road, Port of Spain ☎ 622-7664, is also the Thomas Cook representative, offering eco, cultural and special event tours.

Blue Emperor Tours, 8 Springfield Road, Diego Martin ☎ 637-4246, CTC – Caribbean Travel Company, 7 Saddle Road, Royal Palm Plaza, Maraval ☎ 628-7487. It offers all kinds of tours, excursions, conference travel, ground services and transportation.

Classic Tours and Travel, 36A Maraval Road, Newtown, Port of Spain ☎ 628-5714, offers customized nature, culture, history and lifestyle tours, and is the island's largest cruise ship tour operator.

Kalloo's Sightseeing Tours, 32 Ariapita Avenue, Woodbrook, Port of Spain ☎ 622-9073.

The Travel Centre, Level 2, Up-town Mall, Edward Street, Port of Spain ☎ 625-1636, which offers island tours, nature tours, scuba and golf packages, and other travel arrangements.

Trinidad and Tobago (T&T) Sightseeing Tours, 12 Western Main Road, St. James, Port of Spain ☎ 628-1051, offers attraction, special interest, eco and bird tours to both islands.

Specialist nature tour operators include:

Avifauna Tours ☎ 633-5614

Banwari Experience ☎ 675-1619

Caribbean Discovery Tours ☎ 624-7281

Corkie's Cycle Centre ☎ 622-3970

Kayak Centre ☎ 637-7871

KPE Nature Tours ☎ 637-9664

Nanan's Tours (Caroni Bird Sanctuary) ☎ 645-1305

Nature Tours Unlimted ☎ 665-2683

Palm Tree Tours ☎ 671-2754

Pax Bird Watching Tours ☎ 662-4084

Rooks Nature Tours ☎ 622-8826

South East Eco-Tours, ☎ 644-1072

Trinidad and Tobago Field Naturalists Club, Trinidad – ☎ 645-2132, 624-8017, Tobago – ☎ 639-4276, Ultimate Tours ☎ 643-0912

Wildways Caribbean Adventure Travel ☎ 623-7332

Tobago

Adventure Eco Villas ☎ 639-2839

Classic Tours, Friendship Estate ☎ 639-9891

Cuffie River Nature Retreats ☎ 660-0505

Footprints Eco Resort ☎ 660-0188

Nature Lovers ☎ 639-4559

Sun Fun Tours, 4 Golden Grove Road, Canaan ☎ 639-7461

Tobago Travel, PO Box 163, Scarborough ☎ 639-8778

TELEPHONES

There is direct international calling from most resort hotels although some insist calls are placed through their switchboard and a hefty surcharge is added. For local assistance dial 6211, for overseas help dial 6311 and for directory inquiries dial 6411.

The international dialing code for Trinidad and Tobago is 1 868. From the United States, it is a long distance call – dial 1 868 and the seven digit number. From the United Kingdom dial 010 1 868 and then the seven digit number.

For USA Direct dial 1-800-872-2881, for Call USA dial 1-800-674-7000, for Sprint Express dial 1-800-277-7468, for BT Direct Service, dial 1-800-342-5284, and for Canada Direct dial 1-800-744-2580.

THEATER (THEARE)

Little Carib Theater, White and Roberts Streets, Woodbrook, Port of Spain ☎ 622-4644

Naparima Bowl, 19 Paradise Pasture, San Ferenando ☎ 652-4704

Queen's Hall, St. Ann's Road, Port of Spain ☎ 624-1284

The Space Theater, Bretton Hall, Victoria Avenue, Port of Spain ☎ 623-0732

TIME

Trinidad and Tobago is four hours behind Greenwich Mean Time and on the same time as Eastern Time in the United States. If it is noon in London it is 8am in Trinidad.

While it is important to know the time so that you don't miss your flight, time becomes less important the longer you stay on the island. If you order a taxi it will generally be early or arrive on time, and if you have a business meeting it will start on schedule, for almost everything else be prepared to adopt 'Caribbean time', especially in bars, restaurants and shops. Do not confuse this relaxed attitude with laziness or rudeness, it is just the way things are done in the islands, and the quicker you accept this, the sooner you will start to relax and enjoy yourselves.

TIPPING

Tips are not generally added to bills but it is customary to tip bell-hops in hotels, taxi drivers, guides and other people providing a service. Tip taxi drivers around 10-15% and bell hops TT$6-12 for each piece of luggage.

TOURIST INFORMATION

Trinidad
Tourism and Industrial Development Company of Trinidad and Tobago, 10-14 Philipps Street, Port of Spain, Trinidad ☎ 623-1932/6022

Tobago
IDC Mall, Sangster's Hill, Scarborough, Tobago ☎ 639-4333.

NIB Mall, Scarborough, Tobago ☎ 639-2125

There are information desks at Piarco, Trinidad and Crown Point, Tobago airports.

Overseas

Canada
The RMR Group, Taurus House, 512 Duplex Avenue, Toronto M4R 2ES ☎ (416) 485-8724

Germany
Am Schleifweg 16, D-55128, Maintz ☎ (49) 06131-73337

UK
Morris Kevan International, Mitre House, 66 Abbey Road, Enfield, Middlesex EN1 2QE
☎ 208-350-1015

WEDDINGS

New laws have now made it easier to get married on Trinidad or Tobago. You have to be registered as having been on the island for three days before you can legally marry. This residency period starts the first full day after you arrive. If you decide to get married, there are many hotels that will take care of all the details, and many have idyllic venues for the ceremony and offer honeymoon packages. You must:

Register your arrival at the Registrar's Office, Red House, Abercromby Street, Port of Spain ☎ 623-2450, or on Tobago at either the Registrar General's Office, Jerningham Street, Scarborough ☎ 639-3210, or the Warden's Office, TIDCO Mall, Scarborough ☎ 639-2410.

Three days later you can apply for a Special Marriage Licence (TT$330). You will have to present your passport for identification plus proof if you are divorced or widowed. As the licence is processed in Trinidad it takes two or three working days before it is issued.

YACHTS, CHARTER AND PRIVATE MOORINGS

Trinidad and Tobago is one of the best places for yacht cruising in the Caribbean with excellent waters, good winds, full facilities and lower prices. Although other Caribbean yachting destinations might spring more readily to mind, the 'undiscovered' islands offer several advantages the others do not. Above all, they are outside the active hurricane zone thus allowing year round sailing and cruising, with a significant effect on insurance premiums. Tobago in particular, offers outstanding anchorages close to unspoiled, secluded beaches. The islands also have efficient and economic outhaul and long-term storage facilities, professional machine shops, local repair services and chandleries, plus the benefits of tax and VAT free services, and duty free imported spare parts.

The islands have a long boat building tradition and locally grown teak is of the highest quality and much cheaper than that available in the UK and US, and parts can be custom cast in bronze and zinc, or custom fabricated in fiber glass, aluminum and stainless steel.

Tobago hosts the Angostura/Yachting World Regatta Race Week in May every year, and 'the friendly regatta' is a very popular event which combines competitive racing with fun and relaxation, and there is a wide range of vessels and crews for charter for sailing, sightseeing, fishing and diving. The Trinidad and Tobago Yachting Association has a busy schedule of weekend races between November and June. Visiting vessels are generally welcome to take part, and if you don't have your own yacht, there are often opportunities to sign on as crew.

Boat yards, clubs and marinas include:

CrewsInn is a 66-slip marina and hotel complex with restaurant and shopping. Facilities include a 4-acre boatyard, 200 metric ton travel lift and 60-ton crane.

Industrial Marine Services (IMS), First Avenue, Chaguaramas, Trinidad, which offers a full service haul-out and storage yard with 70-ton marine hoist. Facilities include a paint shop, chandlery, sail-maker, laundry, restaurant with bar, office services and multi-lingual staff ☎ 634-4337

James Wilson and Co, Carenage, Port of Spain ☎ 634-4502

Peake Yacht Services, Chaguaramas Bay, Trinidad, is a full service marina with 150 ton marine hoist capable of beams up to 31ft (9.5m), with 21 in-water berths, security, 10 room hotel, restaurant and bar. laundromat, hot showers, storage and skilled maintenance ☎ 634-4423.

Point Gourde Yachting Centre, Chaguaramas, Trinidad, is a full service marina with 65 in-water berths ☎ 627-5680

Power Boats Mutual Facilities, Chaguaramas Bay, Trinidad, has haul-out and storage, a 50-ton marine hoist, 23 in-water berths, marine supplies, restaurant and bar, ice, office services, wood-working, fiberglass repairs, welding, painting, boat storage, laundromat, fuel, apartments, groceries and showers ☎ 634-4303.

Trinidad and Tobago Yacht Club, Bayshore, close to downtown Port of Spain, has 60 in-water berths, security, restaurant and bar, and laundry ☎ 637-4260

Trinidad and Tobago Yachting Association, Hart's Cut, Chaguaramas Bay, Trinidad, has a full service haul-out yard, 15-ton marine hoist, moorings, bar and snack bar, office services, laundry, repair shed and superb anchorage ☎ 634-4376

Sailing charters are offered by:

Kalina Cats	☎ 639-6306
Loafer Cruises	☎ 639-7312
Natural Mystic	☎ 639-7245

INDEX

INDEX

LANDMARK
VISITORS GUIDES

US & British Virgin Islands

US & British VI*
ISBN: 1 901522 03 2
256pp,
UK £11.95 US $15.95

Antigua & Barbuda

Antigua & Barbuda*
ISBN: 1 901522 02 4
96pp,
UK £5.95 US $12.95

Bermuda

Bermuda*
ISBN: 1 901522 07 5
160pp,
UK £7.95 US $12.95

Barbados

Barbados*
ISBN: 1 901522 32 6
144pp,
UK £6.95 US $12.95

St Lucia

St Lucia*
ISBN: 1 901522 82 2
144pp,
UK £6.95 US $13.95

Pack 2 months into 2 weeks with your Landmark Visitors Guides

Jamaica

Jamaica*
ISBN: 1 901522 31 8
144pp
UK £6.95 US $12.95

The Bahamas

Bahamas*
ISBN: 1 901522 00 8
144pp,
UK £7.95 US $12.95

Florida: Gulf Coast

Florida: Gulf Coast*
ISBN: 1 901522 01 6
160pp
UK £7.95 US $12.95

Florida: The Keys

Florida: The Keys*
ISBN: 1 901522 21 0
160pp,
UK £7.95 US $12.95

Orlando & Central Florida

Orlando*
ISBN: 1 901522 22 9
256pp,
UK £9.95 US $15.95

Dominican Republic

Dominican Republic*
ISBN: 1 901522 08 3
160pp,
UK £7.95 US $12.95

Gran Canaria

Gran Canaria*
ISBN: 1 901522 19 9
160pp
UK £7.95 US $12.95

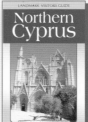

Northern Cyprus

North Cyprus
ISBN: 1 901522 51 2
192pp
UK £8.95

Madeira

Madeira
ISBN: 1 901522 42 3
192pp,
UK £8.95